Taking the IB CP Forward

Edited by
Judith Fabian, Mary Hayden and Jeff Thompson

A John Catt Publication

First Published 2017

by John Catt Educational Ltd,
12 Deben Mill Business Centre, Old Maltings Approach,
Melton, Woodbridge IP12 1BL

Tel: +44 (0) 1394 389850 Fax: +44 (0) 1394 386893
Email: enquiries@johncatt.com
Website: www.johncatt.com

ISBN: 978 1911382 34 8

This book is dedicated to Chris Mannix whose belief, commitment, persistence and creativity enabled a vision to become a reality

1955–2014

Contents

Part C: Implementing the Career-related Programme in an international context

Foreword

While preparation for college or university is an established goal of most post-16 programmes of formal education, debate has long raged about how best to educate young people who do not want to follow an academic route but who wish to pursue a career-related pathway. National systems vary in the extent to which they have engaged with this debate, and the success with which they have educated their young for a range of options post-16 and for the world of work. Career-related or vocational education is regarded in many countries as secondary to the academic preparation required for entry to university, but not in all. Some countries have recognised the pressing needs not only of their economy, businesses and industries, but the needs of their young people who know which careers they wish to follow and, even if they are not sure, want to learn the practical and social skills and attitudes necessary to be successful in the world of work. International education has traditionally not engaged with this debate at all. Programmes offered in international schools, such as A Levels, Advanced Placement and the IB Diploma Programme (DP), are all designed to qualify students for colleges and universities in whichever country they wish to study. Career-related education has been left to local, national institutions.

It is against this backdrop that the IB introduced its fourth programme of international education. The Career-related Programme (CP) combines in two years of study the academic rigour of DP courses, career-related studies organised by the school, often with certification from external providers, and the values and principles of the IB as expressed through the core components of the CP and the IB Learner Profile. It is unique in the world of international education and unique to some national systems of education. The CP is a flexible, inclusive programme that can be adapted to local and national contexts and, most importantly, adapted to the needs of individual students with a wide range of abilities and needs and interests.

The IB launched the CP as recently as 2012. It was a bold step but one that had the support of many in the IB community who had been asking for a programme of international education to meet the needs of students, post-16. Many of these students were being educated through the IB's Primary and Middle Years Programmes and then, at the age of 16, found themselves stranded – wanting to continue in international education but not having a programme that would meet their needs. The mantra of inclusiveness in international education has served students up to the age of 16 reasonably well, but less so those students entering post-16 education.

Following the tradition of IB programmes originating with visionary and brave teachers, the CP was born in the snowy north of Finland, in a state-funded college that wanted to offer an international education to its Finnish business studies students. It was soon joined by a college in Quebec, Canada, that aimed to internationalise the education of their police studies students, and then by a small group of enthusiastic national and international schools in Europe and the Middle East who overcame many obstacles to pilot an unknown and untried programme. While the IB was cautious about the development of a hybrid programme that included career-related qualifications designed by non-IB providers, the enthusiasm of this small group of pilot schools convinced it to commit to the development of what became the CP.

This book comprises views, perceptions and opinions concerning ways in which the CP can be implemented, and the impact it can have on a school and its students. The contributors are school leaders, programme coordinators, teachers – many from the pilot group of CP schools – and IB staff who have been working with the programme since its conception. They are all part of a group of pioneers who championed the CP to administrators, governors, political leaders, higher education institutions, employers, parents and to the students themselves. They are eager to share their experiences, reflections and thoughts about the challenges and successes of these first years of the CP so that more schools may consider offering it and more students may benefit.

The book is organised in three distinct parts. Part A sets out the context of the CP in terms of a description of the programme by Dominic Robeau, the IB's Senior Curriculum Manager responsible for the CP, followed by a discussion of the key issues around recognition of the CP by higher education institutions and employers (Forbes). Chapters follow on key components of the CP core – Personal and Professional Skills (Wyten), Service Learning (Berger Kaye), the Reflective Project (Daneau) and Language Development (Juniper, Woodcock, Dietrich, Worth and Phipps-Orive) – components which serve to integrate the whole programme and which embody the value and principles of an IB education.

Part B comprises a series of chapters on how the CP has been implemented in state-funded schools and how it has impacted these schools and their students in the US (Campbell and Deflorian), the UK (Barrs, Smith, Greig), and Australia (Carozza). The contributors write about the the power of the CP to change young lives in challenging communities, the value of schools working together, and the fruitful collaboration that can take place between universities and CP schools for the benefit of students of all abilities.

Part C focuses on the CP in international schools. These schools have experienced significant successes and some challenges in implementing a sustainable CP that addresses the needs of their students, including the most able, who are focused on career-related pathways and not on traditional academic routes. The schools range from one of the oldest international schools, the International School of Geneva (de Wilde), to more recently established schools in Berlin (Kotrc and Peters), Dubai (Worth), and Hong Kong (Redden). The final chapter in Part C (Bastable) is written by a former head of one of the schools in the first CP pilot group, and conveys the enthusiasm and commitment of those pioneer schools to what they intrinsically believed was the best way to meet not only the needs of their students, but also to raise their aspirations and help them achieve their dreams.

It is our intention that readers across a wide range of educational contexts will find the experiences and thoughts of these contributors to be of interest, support and encouragement in their search for the best education for 16 year old students with a range of abilities and interests. We also hope that school leaders and teachers who are currently involved in the CP will find ideas and suggestions here that will stimulate their own work, serve the learning needs of their students and help meet some of the needs of the communities in which they live.

Many people have been involved in the production off this book. We wish to express our deep gratitude and appreciation to them all; to the contributors who have demonstrated professional knowledge and skill in sharing with us insights borne of their experience and commitment to career-related education, and in exercising enormous patience in responding so generously to editorial demands, and to our colleagues in John Catt Educational Limited for their continued guidance and encouragement throughout a process in which we, as editors, feel privileged to have played a part.

Judith Fabian

Mary Hayden

Jeff Thompson

About the contributors

David Barrs is Co-Head-teacher at the Anglo European School, a state-funded, comprehensive school in Essex, UK which implemented the CP in 2010. David became the first chairperson of the Association for Citizenship Teaching in the UK when it was launched in June 2001. He also advises the United Nations Association on educational matters, and in 1995 edited the UN Kits which first introduced him to the IB. David is director of the UK IB Schools and Colleges Association (IBSCA) and has served on the IB Heads Council, becoming its chair in 2015 and serving on the IB Board of Governors.

John Bastable left the UK for a two-year teaching post overseas and returned thirty-eight years later having gained extensive international experience. Working initially in Germany, he travelled on to Sardinia, Papua New Guinea, India, Dubai and Jordan, spending 35 years in leadership positions. He was the founding director of two schools offering IB programmes, and participated in piloting and establishing the CP. Throughout his career, John has supported the policy of inclusion in international schools. He is now semi-retired in Cambridge offering consultancy on matters of culture and school security and is a governor of a school for students with special needs.

Cathryn Berger Kaye is an international education consultant who works with schools world-wide on service learning, effective approaches to teaching and learning, social and emotional development, school climate and culture, youth engagement and leadership, and advisory programmes. She has been a long-time consultant with the IB, assisting with Service Learning in the CP and the DP as a key contributor to the new CAS Guide and support materials. A former teacher, Cathryn is the author of the widely used book *The Complete Guide to Service Learning*, and two books co-authored with environmental advocate, Philippe Cousteau.

Paul Campbell has worked for the IB organisation in the Americas region in numerous capacities. Since 1988 he has assisted hundreds of schools and school systems in implementing and sustaining IB programmes. He has been involved in creating the global IB Educators Network, the IB's services to US school districts, and advocacy work with universities and governments. He currently serves as the Head of Development and Outreach at IB's global centre in Washington, DC. He lives in Maryland with his wife, an archaeologist and specialist in historic preservation, and his daughter, a DP student at Albert Einstein High School.

John Carozza is Head of DP group 6 subjects at Queensland Academy for Creative Industries (QACI) in Brisbane Australia. He has taught film for over 25 years. as well as being a practising artist. Over his career he has taught DP Theatre and Visual Arts, and established film and TV courses in schools in Queensland. John established the career-related pathway for the CP at QACI in

2013, along with acting as a CP consultant for other schools in the South Pacific region. He has also worked as a consultant in the creative industries as well as lecturing in World Cinema Studies at Queensland University of Technology (QUT) and Griffith Film School, Queensland.

Patrick Daneau has been a philosophy and a DP Theory of Knowledge (TOK) teacher for 16 years at Collège François-Xavier-Garneau, located in Quebec City, Canada. For more than eight years he has been leading TOK workshops across Canada and in Africa. He has been involved with the development and implementation of the CP from the very beginning and is the moderator of the CP Reflective Project for the IB.

Natasha Deflorian joined the IB in August 2010 after teaching English in both North and South America. She has experience working with all four IB programmes and currently serves as the global manager of pre-authorisation services. From 2011 to 2016 Natasha served as the CP Associate Manager for the Americas region and supported the authorisation of the first 100 CP schools in that region. In her previous role at the IB, she worked closely with a variety of schools, educational systems and leaders, and developed a deep understanding of career and technical education and the benefits for students as they become lifelong learners in a global society.

Conan de Wilde is a DP graduate who went on to study at Oxford University and the Open University. After leaving university, he developed an interest in woodworking, construction, and professional education. He was a teacher and a head of department before being appointed as the CP coordinator at the Campus des Nations of the International School of Geneva a post which he held until July, 2015. He is currently the Assistant Principal (Academic) at the La Grande Boissière Campus of the International School of Geneva.

Ramona Dietrich is the Language Development Coordinator at Oeiras International School, Portugal. In addition to teaching English within the Language Development component she is also currently teaching English Language Acquisition and Drama in the MYP. She is an educational technology enthusiast and works toward creating a classroom environment that promotes life-long learning. Ramona believes that the IB Learner Profile paves the way for a successful future.

Judith Fabian taught English and Drama in secondary schools in London followed by 15 years as department head and principal in international schools in Jordan, Tanzania and Germany. She joined the IB in Cardiff in 2004 as Head of Programme Development, and in 2007 was appointed Chief Academic Officer leading the development of IB curriculum for students aged 3 to 19 years. Latterly based in the IB centre in The Hague, she left the IB in 2014 to return to her home in the UK to work as an educational consultant, editor and author. She has presented to and worked with schools and educators all over the world.

Theresa Forbes is an international educator with over 25 years experience working in national and international schools. She has been a senior advisor for the national curriculum for England, Director of the International Primary Curriculum (IPC), and Head of Regional Development for the IB. Theresa has worked as a teacher and head teacher in Indonesia, Oman and the Netherlands. She is the founding director of Shaping Learning and has supported initiatives with the IB, Aga Khan Education Services and Shell. From 2010-2014, Theresa worked as Head of Regional Development for the IB region of Africa, Europe and Middle East (AEM), working with the CP in its early days of piloting, and advocating for government recognition in England, Netherlands, Spain and the United Arab Emirates.

Kate Greig graduated from Birmingham University in the UK in1987 having read English Language and Literature. She trained as a teacher in Manchester before relocating to East Kent to start her teaching career. She took up the post of head teacher at King Ethelbert School in 2009 when the school was under scrutiny for being a poor performing school. Progress measures now place King Ethelbert as one of the top performing schools in England, and Kate and the staff continue to drive forward the aspirations and expectations for all the students.

Mary Hayden is Head of the Department of Education at the University of Bath, where she is a member of the Internationalisation and Globalisation of Education Research Group. Her research interests relate to international schools and international education, an area in which she has published widely in research journals and books, as well as supervising Masters and Doctoral students and leading a number of major research projects. She is Editor-in-Chief of the Journal of Research in International Education, a Founding Trustee of the Alliance for International Education and a member of the advisory boards of a number of international education projects.

Alexandra Juniper graduated from Kings College London and the London School of Economics after studying Chemistry and Philosophy of Science. She was appointed as a DP Chemistry and TOK teacher in Aloha College Spain in 1990. She also taught and co-ordinated the DP at Rydal Penrhos in North Wales before moving to the International School of Geneva, Campus des Nations, in 2011 to run the DP programme there. In 2014 she combined DP coordination with CP coordination and is now in charge of both programmes at the school. Alex continues to teach Chemistry and TOK, and also examines and writes IB examination papers for DP chemistry.

Peter Kotrc is Austrian. He taught his first DP class in 1980 and has been a committed supporter of the IB philosophy ever since. After leadership roles at Vienna International School and The International School of The Hague, he is currently Director/CEO of Berlin Brandenburg International School which was the first four-programme IB World School.

Julia Peters is British born and grew up in UK, Canada and Germany. After working in the performing arts in a variety of capacities, she moved to the Netherlands and gained a post-graduate certificate in education, having had to learn Dutch very quickly! She has taught English at Berlin Brandenberg International School for ten years, and since 2009 has also been the CP coordinator.

Catheryn Phipps-Orive has been a bilingual instructor for over two decades in both Mexico and the US. In addition to teaching Spanish at the University of Denver for several years, she has taught in the Dual Language Programme at Regis University and taught IB DP courses. She is also an examiner for Spanish Language Acquisition. Additionally, she teaches medical IB Spanish to medical students and health care professionals with Common Ground International. Her teaching focus is on communicative competence in second language acquisition for adult learners, and her research is in the area of cognitive linguistics and identity development in adult learners of second languages.

Stewart Redden has been an IB educator since 1993 and is currently the Vice Principal at Renaissance College in Hong Kong, a four-programme IB World School. Stewart has spent most of his educational career in international schools as an administrator and teacher in Taiwan, Singapore and Spain. He currently contributes to the IB community as a Visiting Team Leader and consultant for both the DP and CP. His philosophy of education is that learning should be a 'flow' experience in which students enjoy the challenge of developing new skills and remain effective learners throughout their lives.

Dominic Robeau is the Senior Curriculum Manager for the CP and was responsible for writing all of the new 2016 CP guides and resources. He was also responsible for the writing of the 2015 IB Diploma CAS (Creativity, Activity, and Creativity) guide. Experienced in the MYP, DP and CP, Dominic has many years of classroom and educational leadership experience in local and international schools in Australia, Indonesia and the United Arab Emirates. A secondary English Literature teacher by training, he holds his Masters in English Literature and Communications from Murdoch University, Australia, and a Masters in Educational Leadership and Management from Newcastle University, Australia.

Tony Smith worked in Essex, UK, in high schools and comprehensive schools as a teacher of English, a Head of Department and a Deputy Head, before becoming head teacher of Dartford Grammar School, Kent in 1986. Dartford Grammar School was authorised as an IB World School offering the DP in 1996, and introduced the MYP in 2014. Tony was a member of the steering committee of IBSCA, and chaired it from 2007 to 2009. Since leaving headship, he has worked as a consultant on school improvement and curriculum development for a variety of organisations, including Kent County Council, and individual schools.

Jeff Thompson is Emeritus Professor of Education at the University of Bath with particular teaching and research interests in the fields of international schools and international education. He has published many articles and books in this area, in which he also teaches and supervises Doctoral and Masters students. He has been involved with the IB since its earliest days in a number of roles, including Academic Director, Chair of the Examining Board and Head of Research. He is a member of a wide range of advisory boards for international education projects and holds governance positions for a number of schools.

Sara Woodcock is currently the CP coordinator at the Anglo European School (AES) in Essex, UK. She is an examiner for the IB, as well as an IB school visitor and consultant. Sara spent seven years working for the British Council in Madrid before joining AES, and prior to that worked as a lecturer at a Sixth Form college in Gloucestershire.

Mike Worth began teaching in 1985 in the UK following seven years working in industry. Teaching Art and Design in a secondary school and then a college of Further Education, helped to develop in him a keen interest and commitment to different ways of learning. In 1995 Mike moved to Australia as part of a teacher exchange programme specialising in vocational education. Mike has been an examiner for the New South Wales HSC (Higher School Certificate) Curriculum and also written a number of text books. A move to Dubai in 2009 to join an IB school brought him to the new CP in the early stages of its development. Mike is now an CP workshop leader and consultant.

Part A

Overview of the Career-related Programme

Chapter 1

An introduction to the Career-related Programme

Dominic Robeau

The rationale for the Career-related Programme (CP)

The status of career-related education in many countries is changing, with the growing understanding that in order to achieve greater economic strength young people need to be able to acquire and apply practical skills as well as academic knowledge. Through a career-related education, students are both encouraged and expected to develop a greater range of personal capacities that expand, rather than limit, their future occupational options. Further, there is a growing realisation in both developed and underdeveloped countries that, given the benefits of a good career-related education, it should be available not only for the less able students but for all students.

The introduction of the CP is a significant milestone in the history of the International Baccalaureate (IB) in that it seeks to broaden access to an IB education and bridge the academic/career-related study divide. The CP incorporates the vision and educational principles of the IB into a unique programme, specifically developed for students who wish to engage in career-related learning, as opposed to purely academic studies. The CP's flexible educational framework allows schools to meet the needs of their students, and enables each school to create its own distinctive version of the programme fitted to the backgrounds of the students and the local contexts. A significant feature of the programme is that it provides sufficient flexibility to allow for local differences.

The programme is aimed at the growing number of countries which set out to develop programmes based on the realisation that today's youth are seeking alternative educational and career pathways not found in the broad generalist, and largely academic, programmes offered in many educational systems. Not only does the CP meet this rising demand for alternative approaches to post-16 education, it also meets the demand for academic rigour, which in turn ensures the CP as a whole provides articulated pathways upon secondary graduation. In short, students entering the CP are cognisant of the opportunities available to them upon graduation. The breadth of different pathways the CP is currently providing to students around the world indicates that the CP is designed for those students who seek a higher education, but also provides for students who are interested in internships, apprenticeships, technical/community colleges or the world of work, thus seeking to meet the growing demand of employers for specialised skills in differing fields.

It is worth mentioning at this point that the IB has, for the purpose of ensuring a collective term for career-related education, noted the following as belonging under this term: apprenticeship training, technical education, applied education, occupational education, career-focused education, university foundation programmes, vocational education, VET (vocational education and training), TVET (technical and vocational education and training), CVET (continuing vocational education and training) and CTE (career and technical education).

The nature of the CP

The CP is grounded in the mission, the educational principles and the Learner Profile of the IB. Through the CP, students have access to a broad, flexible education that will give them the knowledge, practical skills, intellectual engagement and international mindedness to succeed in higher education and tomorrow's global workplace. The CP provides a high standard of international education through its provision of IB Diploma Programme (DP) courses and what is referred to as the CP core, which consists of components that link the DP courses with the career-related study: Personal and Professional Skills; Language Development; Service Learning and the Reflective Project. All these elements of the programme are developed by the IB. Additionally, the programme provides direct access to local, national and international higher education institutions with its requirement of a locally, or internationally, accredited career-related study. Schools choose or develop their own specific career-related studies to meet students' needs and in order to enhance the opportunities for their students upon graduation.

CP graduates meet the four key areas identified by David T. Conley (Conley, 2010) as prerequisites for further/higher education readiness: key cognitive strategies; academic behaviours; academic knowledge; learning skills and techniques. CP students are immersed in specific academic and career-related studies which lead to a high degree of understanding of complex concepts and knowledge. Further, CP students develop skills and knowledge underpinned by international mindedness, highlighted by Conley as critical contextual skills and awareness to ensure application and acculturation to further/higher education. Educators have been quick to recognise the value and benefits of the CP for a wide range of students, but it is interesting to note that, to date, the vast majority of CP graduates have continued on to further and higher education rather than directly into work.

That the CP can be applied in any country, for any student, further broadens its appeal for both schools and students. The CP is well placed to respond to local, regional and national strategies and labour markets by providing specific post-graduation pathways, for example in media, business or hospitality, in order to create a professional and employable workforce. The flexibility and mobility of the CP mean that it can be adapted to suit specific needs and yet, at the same time, provide a breadth of alternative pathways suitable for a changing market.

The CP takes into account global trends of future industries by being combined with specific career-related studies. Specialisation of career related pathways can also be cost effective, allowing a growing economy to develop in a rational and progressive manner.

In the US, schools are delivering the CP in healthcare, engineering, business and other specific career-related pathways. The rapid growth of US schools delivering the CP points to a strong need for a career-related programme that brings with it the educational ethos and principles of an IB education. Based on the take-up of the CP thus far across the US, the growth of the programme seems likely to be significant and influential in the coming years.

In the UK, the variety of pathways on offer point to a diverse application of the CP, meeting the needs of a student population intent on specialising in specific career-related pathways. For example, schools are undertaking the CP in areas such as business, sports management, and childcare to name just a few. Using the CP, schools have found they are able to attract students who may not have continued in a school setting, leading to greater retainment of students in education. In turn, students are provided with the support structures of a high school that are not readily accessible elsewhere.

International schools are also discovering the benefits of the CP as it provides them with pathways that may not be accessible to their students in the local context. For example, a student in an international school seeking a career-related focus in their final two years of school may not be able to access local institutions due to language limitations or legal requirements. A school offering the CP can retain such a student and provide a specific pathway for the student to follow, leading to successful placement upon graduation in an area of their choice. The CP is thus able to provide international school students with greater opportunities post high school; opportunities that previously they may have had to seek in their home countries.

By February 2017 there were 140 authorised CP schools, with a further 100 in candidacy (the process of applying to implement the CP), in 22 countries around the world. The widespread growth of popularity of the CP indicates its inherent value and, as such, points to a robust future.

A brief history of the CP

The CP originated in the city of Oulu in northern Finland from an IB project later to become known as the pilot partnership model. In early 2002, the IB was approached by Oulu Vocational College, a non-IB school and one of the largest vocational schools in Finland. The college was keen to embrace the educational philosophy of the IB and deliver DP courses to its students. With a strategic aim of broadening access to an IB education, the IB readily agreed to a meeting involving IB staff, the Finland Ministry of Education and representatives from Oulu Vocational College and Oulun Lyseo Lukio, a local authorised IB Diploma Programme school. At this landmark meeting, it was established that the divide between vocational and academic education needed to be bridged to allow students the best opportunities possible in vocational education. It was reasoned that students undertaking vocational courses of study would benefit from the challenge, rigour and academic nature of DP courses. Further, it was decided that a model resembling that of the DP core (Theory of Knowledge; Creativity, Activity and Service; the Extended Essay) could be applied to the envisaged programme of study for Finnish vocational students. The Finnish Board of Education showed considerable support for this project, both financially and through its active involvement in the steering group. With growing excitement at the possible opportunities for students globally accessing this programme, the IB worked hard to ensure the project would be implemented.

The project began in 2004 with the first cohort of 24 students following the Finnish national vocational qualification in business and administration, supplemented by DP courses. In the following two years the IB researched and evaluated this educational framework. It proved to be somewhat challenging for some DP practitioners who considered it to be a departure from what was considered to be an IB education; for some, seeing DP courses combined with vocational studies did not sit well, arguing that the IB had no business being involved in vocational education and that the DP would suffer by association. However, within the IB, and in the IB community, a core group of determined educators saw the future and proceeded to move apace. They reasoned that such a framework would meet the rising global demand for a form of international education that would bridge the academic/vocational divide, respond to the IB's mission, and provide greater access to an IB education. They believed that the final programme would be of benefit to a growing number of countries who were finding that their young people were seeking more practical, work-focused pathways in education. The underlying principle of the framework was that it would provide students with career-orientated pathways combined with a sound academic IB education.

A key focus of the group's research was the definition of the word vocational and its various permutations globally. It was found that the term 'vocational' was limiting the potential of the career-focused, third element of the educational framework devised for the project. Instead of 'vocational study', it was decided that the term 'career-related study' would be used to encompass all the types of education that had a specific career focus. An agreed model was developed during these early pilot years, resulting in an educational framework of three parts: a minimum of two DP courses; an IB designed CP core; and a career-related study, to be chosen by the school.

The CP core was designed to bridge students' chosen DP courses and their career-related studies, enabling students to enhance their personal and interpersonal development and develop the skills and competencies required for lifelong learning as well as providing a strong international dimension. The three components of the CP core consisted, at that time, of a Reflective Project, focused on an ethical dilemma; Community and Service; and an Approaches to Learning course which focused on developing students' skills through four themes: thinking; personal development; communication; intercultural awareness. These three components were understood to be at the heart of the CP educational framework which, in 2006, became officially known as the International Baccalaureate Career-related Certificate (IBCC), but which for clarity will be referred to using the title it later acquired, the Career-related Programme, the IBCP.

Another milestone occurred in 2006 when Collège Garneau, a state-funded academic institution located in Quebec City, Canada, became the first DP school outside Finland to begin trialling the CP. The school offered two pathways, one for students planning on university studies after a two-year study programme (including the DP), and one for students preparing for a place in the labour market after a three-year study programme. In this college, the CP was connected to the local qualification of Police Studies and studied over three years.

In 2008, North Karelia College, a vocational college located in Outokumpu, Finland, joined the CP partnership model pilot. The college partnered with an IB World School, Joensuun Lyseon Lukio, which provided the teachers for the DP courses. The vocational qualification offered by North Karelia College was in audio-visual communications, a Finnish vocational qualification that allowed students to find work in Finland and abroad.

In the years that followed, up to 2011, 12 DP schools in the US, UK, Germany, Thailand and United Arab Emirates also began trialling the CP. A number of meetings were held to discuss the CP with these schools, resulting in the addition of a language acquisition course forming part of the CP framework instead of the original requirement for a Language B (the title then given to language acquisition courses in the DP) course as one of the two DP courses. In 2011, after lengthy and complex discussions with stakeholders and extended analysis of the requirement for a language acquisition course in the CP framework, the language acquisition requirement was restructured as a component of the CP core, effective from 2012, and renamed Language Development. Adding Language Development to the core would reflect the value placed by the IB on the deep connection between language learning and international-mindedness.

The IB sought to expand the Finnish partnership model pilot, and in 2009 selected seven non-IB schools in the county of Kent, UK, under the mentorship of Dane Court Grammar School, a well-established DP school. The goal of this pilot was to provide new and significant opportunities for both the schools and the students. In 2010 the IB, with Dane Court, began a series of meetings and professional development workshops with all seven schools to prepare them for the implementation of the CP. Supported by Kent County Council, which provided funding to support the schools, the pilot began in 2011 with the first five of seven schools implementing the CP. In 2012, the remaining two schools joined the pilot. Noting the success of the pilot, in 2014 a further two schools in Kent began implementing the CP under the mentorship of Dane Court. As a direct result of the success of the CP in these pilot schools, a further 18 schools in Kent will be authorised to implement the programme in 2017 as IB World Schools (see chapters 9 and 10 on the Kent pilot).

The relationship model pilot was not confined to Finland and the UK. In 2012, three schools in Mexico expressed a strong interest in the pilot and in 2013, two non-IB schools, Bachillerato UPAEP Huamantla and Bachillerato UPAEP Tehuacán implemented the CP under the mentorship of Bachillerato UPAEP Santiago, a DP school. The success of this relationship model led to the two schools applying to be CP candidate schools in 2016.

The success of the relationship model pilot is evident in the school self-study reports (the reports schools write on their progress as part of the IB school evaluation process) where the authors concluded that the CP has been of strong benefit for the students. North Karelia College, Finland, noted: "We have witnessed a change in our organisation due to teaching and developing the CP. The students studying in, and graduating from, the international programme have been more international and open-minded than our mainstream students." The Kent partnership schools corroborated this view: "The CP is enhancing students' aspirations and employability". The head of one Kent school spoke passionately at a CP conference in 2012 on the benefits of introducing the CP to her school, noting that it has had "an enormous impact on both the school and the students".

In November 2010 the governing body of the IB finally approved the implementation of the CP from September 2012, in authorised IB World Schools that offer the DP. A process for CP authorisation was established and within a short period a further 40 schools, predominantly in the UK and the US, were authorised to implement the CP.

Recognition and accreditation

The IB is committed to a full and comprehensive range of activities designed to support recognition and wider awareness of the programme; this includes continuing to secure government recognition and/or accreditation in those countries where accreditation is a requirement to enable schools to offer the programme. In October 2011 the IB submitted the CP to Ofqual (Office of Qualifications and Examinations Regulation), the regulator of qualifications, examinations and assessments in England, for accreditation. By achieving this recognition, the programme would become more attractive to English schools as an accredited certificate and it would allow the IB to promote the CP in other countries as an established English certificate, encouraging independent accreditation in those countries. Ofqual duly accredited the CP without reservation.

Building on the success of the Ofqual accreditation, in 2012 the CP was submitted to the Young People's Learning Agency (YPLA) in England for the provision of state school funding. YPLA is sponsored by the Department for Education and is mandated to provide public funding to English state-funded schools. In 2012 funding for the CP was approved by the YPLA. This was another milestone for the CP in that it allowed state schools in England to claim funding for the delivery of the CP. Further, in 2012, the Queensland Curriculum and Assessment Authority in Australia accredited the CP's Reflective Project as a contributing study for the Queensland Certificate of Education (QCE). In 2014, the CP was shortlisted for the prestigious World Innovation Summit for Education (WISE) award, which recognises innovative international education projects that transform society.

The fourth programme

After the CP went mainstream as an offering to all DP schools, there was a growing realisation that the programme needed to be more firmly placed within the IB continuum of education for students aged 3 to 19: the Primary Years Programme, the Middle Years Programme and the Diploma Programme. To that end, in November 2014, the IB's governing body approved the change in name of the IBCC to the Career-related Programme (CP). At this landmark meeting the board also approved the CP as a stand-alone programme, meaning that from 2016 non-DP schools could apply to become IB World Schools through becoming authorised to implement the CP. This decision meant that IB students around the world would have access to a flexible, dynamic and rigorous career-related IB educational framework, designed to meet the changing needs of students, universities, and employers.

In early 2014 a CP programme review began in the IB organisation, resulting in the redesign of the four components of the CP core; a complete set of new documents was launched in 2015. Approaches to Learning was renamed Personal and Professional Skills, and Community and Service was renamed Service Learning. The Reflective Project was also reconfigured, resulting in recognition from UCAS (The Universities and Colleges Admissions Service) in the UK, which operates the application process for British universities and which allocated the same number of tariff points to the Reflective Project as the DP's Extended Essay.

The current programme model in Figure 1 shows these new components of the CP and how they relate to one another.

Online facilitated workshops for the Reflective Project coordinator training and Personal and Professional Skills were first made available in 2011 and have since grown in number, allowing participants to choose from either online or face to face workshops on a range of CP topics.

Figure 1: The CP programme model, 2017

The CP has come of age in a world where the need for new pathways in education is increasingly evident. Over the years it has undergone exhaustive processes to ensure that it is fit for purpose and, as the revised CP was implemented in 2016, schools and educators are excited and enthused by the possibilities the programme provides. No more will students have to fit into a formal academic educational system; instead, students can choose those studies that are of most interest, knowing that the combination of the three elements of the framework known as the CP will provide them with the skills and knowledge to enable them to move confidently into the future.

References

Conley, D. T. (2010): *College and Career Ready: Helping All Students Succeed Beyond High School*. San Francisco, California: Jossey-Bass.

Chapter 2

Achieving recognition of the Career-related Programme: the broad view

Theresa Forbes

Introduction and context

In this chapter I will describe how the Career-related Programme (CP) is accepted, recognised, reviewed and positioned by the International Baccalaureate (IB), as well as by different bodies and institutions around the world. I will also consider the barriers and bridges to the success of the CP in helping students to seek a meaningful pathway to higher education (HE) or the world of work. Acknowledgement of an educational programme by organisations and institutions is often referred to as 'recognition', a term used widely in HE and increasingly in the world of work. Recognition will be considered here with regard to the future of the CP and I hope the following reflections will contribute constructively to the success of the CP. I believe that the CP is a pioneering piece of curriculum design, bringing together and equally respecting the international IB components and the national or international career-related studies from a given country or international body. The CP's flexible approach enables the design of authentic, customised and real world learning experiences, all too absent in many post-16 international education programmes.

The context within which the CP is currently positioned is summarised below. It is important to emphasise that, at the time of writing, the CP has largely been implemented in existing IB Diploma Programme (DP) schools, and a few non-DP schools specifically included in the initial pilot phase. Full access for non-DP schools was granted in April 2016, with first teaching of the CP to take place in 2018.

The IB introduced its first programme of international education, the DP, in 1968. The first students sat DP examinations in 1970. In 1994 the Middle Years Programme (MYP) followed and in 1997 the Primary Years Programme (PYP) was added. In 2007, the first schools began to develop and pilot a new offering from the IB: the International Baccalaureate Career-related Certificate (IBCC) as it was first called. From September 2012 the CP (as it became) was offered to all authorised DP schools, opening up a new post-16 IB pathway. The growth of the programmes is outlined in Table 1.

Programme	Year of launch	Number of authorised IB programmes at July 2016	Number of countries
IB Diploma Programme	1968	2795	143
IB Middle Years Programme	1994	1306	104
IB Primary Years Programme	1997	1266	106
IB Career-related Programme	2012	114	21

Table 1: Authorised IB programmes (IB, 2016)

This chapter will provide some perspectives on recognition for the CP and consider the extent to which recognition is the key to CP's success. Success is determined here in terms of:

- uptake – the number of CP authorised schools
- quality – of the education offer
- evidence – of HE institutions and governments that recognise the CP
- student pathways – after graduating with the CP
- partners wishing to collaborate
- advocating employers and industry partners

I will also review the challenges the CP may face in becoming recognised as a new programme and qualification compared with the challenges the DP faced. Will the CP's journey prove to be easier than the journey the DP has taken because the IB is now an established brand? Given the very nature of the CP, it being 'a hybrid qualification' (Davey and Fuller, 2011), I will consider how a combined international and career-related qualification may position itself to be recognised in the field of both international and national education.

Defining recognition

Amongst the many definitions of recognition, the following general definition caters well for recognition in its various forms, and within the context for which the CP, as a programme and a qualification, exists.

"Appreciation or acclaim for an achievement, service or ability" (OUP, 2016)

The CP and all of its component parts add up to a well-rounded and broad programme which needs a full narrative to be understood. Recognition, in the case of educational programmes, has been traditionally seen through a narrower lens than the above definition in terms of how an HE institution will accept an entry level qualification.

Bergen and Hunt (Council of Europe, 2008), describe recognition in the following way:

"Think of recognition as a bridge that learners have to cross in order to move from one education system to another … think of qualifications …. as a suitcase or backpack that has to be carried across the bridge. If the bridge enables learners to cross the divide between two education systems, they may well be faced by a 'customs office' at the other end of the bridge in the shape of regulations and practices for the recognition of their qualifications" (p 7).

Bergen and Hunt describe recognition as a constantly evolving process and also a 'public service'. Their work has focused on the HE dimension of recognition and how the collaboration of different bodies and the development of conventions and agreements has enabled thousands of people to cross the 'bridge' of recognition to enable greater global mobility via education.

Mechanisms and processes such as the Lisbon Recognition Convention (Council of Europe and UNESCO, signed 1997) and the Bologna Process (European Commission, 1999) have given rise to fairer recognition of educational achievement across borders. The Bologna Process aimed to create a European Higher Education Area, in which students can choose from a wide and transparent range of high quality courses, and benefit from 'smooth recognition procedures' (European Commission,1999). However, the good work of the Council of Europe and UNESCO in helping to further the educational opportunities and mobility for all still leaves an absence of an international awarding body or coalition to recognise qualifications more globally. Therefore, the work of gaining recognition at government and HE levels remains a labour intensive process.

In line with the work of the Council of Europe, the IB, across its three regions (African, Europe and the Middle East; the Americas; and Asia Pacific), places most of its focus on securing recognition statements from HE institutions, predominantly for the DP, and latterly the CP and MYP. The IB focuses on developing new opportunities to educate HE institutions and governments about its programmes but it currently does not explicitly define what it means by 'recognition' in its own literature and website. Such practice means the IB has a clear focus on developing relationships and agreements with HE institutions, a direction that no one would dispute, but now that the IB has four programmes and has introduced a career-related offer, it is important to consider more specifically other stakeholders who need to recognise the CP's contribution and value.

A broader view of recognition

Recognition has layers of complexity that will have differing levels of importance for different stakeholders. For the purposes of this chapter, HE and government recognition will still be prioritised, but if there is one main take-away from this chapter it will be that we should look more broadly at recognition to reach other important internal and external stakeholders.

The nature of recognition and the value of qualifications is changing with the advent of the customisation of qualifications by corporate entities which are beginning to develop their own branded and accredited courses. Such initiatives are being developed because many organisations wish to be more selective in the skill-sets of their employees and will, therefore, customise and develop their own qualifications to meet their needs. Helping employers understand new qualifications will require a different approach to recognition than that used for HE and governments. Different stakeholders will require different access points in their understanding of a programme or qualification. They will go through a series of stages or ask questions specific to their needs before accepting a new qualification, either as a consumer of it, or a body needing to accredit it, or an employer trying to understand it.

It may be helpful to consider the process stakeholders go though when accepting a new educational offer or initiative. One could look at recognition in terms of what I will describe as the four 'As' to give focus to some of the phases key decision-makers and validators of a new product will go through. In turn, different actions will be needed to respond to these phases:

- **Awareness** requires the development of orientation opportunities with an identified range of stakeholders

- **Acceptance** requires a level of understanding of the qualification's worth and purpose as a new contender and how it meets an individual or strategic agenda

- **Adoption** requires both philosophical alignment and financial commitment

- **Advocacy** requires experienced users to share their success stories and outcomes

A range of individuals and bodies, internal and external to IB, will need to understand more fully what happens in the minds of those stakeholders who will be on their own journey to recognising CP; Awareness, Acceptance, Adoption, and Advocacy are critical stages that external stakeholders will go though. Traditionally, within the IB and other competitor academic qualifications, the providers have placed their efforts on HE institutions and governments, but the stakeholders listed in Table 2 may need to engage more fully with a broader view of recognition and different strategies for a career-related future.

CP key stakeholders	
Internal IB stakeholders	**External IB stakeholders**
IB Board and sub-committees	CP Students
IB Senior Leadership Team	CP Schools
Relevant IB staff	Career-related partners/providers
IB Regional/Global staff	Employers/Corporate
IB Communications and marketing	Higher and Further Education Institutions
IB helpdesk	Governments

Table 2: Key stakeholders in the CP

In highlighting a greater group of stakeholders I am trying to shine a light on how complex it may be to cascade the right messages about the CP to wider audiences. It is clear that the CP narrative is one that is more complex to explain than the other IB programmes, so assuming the CP is considered a worthwhile offer, the challenge here is how to make recognition the responsibility of more members of the IB community and to widen the current focus from HE to other critical stakeholders.

The nature of the CP and recognition of its value

The IB is the first organisation to attempt to bridge not only an academic and career-related divide, but also a national and an international divide, in one offer. The CP is unique in its structure in that it has interdependence with a career-related offer from other providers to make up its whole. The CP may be best described as a 'hybrid qualification' serving both the academic and the career-related domains and, thus, across the range of qualifications available to the 16-19 age range, the CP is emerging as a new and different offer. Davey and Fuller describe a hybrid qualification in the following way:

> 'Any kind of combination of general (academic) and vocational learning provided for those aged 14 plus' (Davey and Fuller, 2011).

The hybrid nature of the CP provides an opportunity to link and collaborate with a range of education systems to provide a blend of academic and career-related studies. In addition, alongside developing international understanding, the national needs of a country at governmental level can also be met through the design of the CP. As a consequence, the CP should begin to open up new access routes for students. Through the CP, the IB will engage with different types of learning institutions and student pathways, and this will lead to opportunities for different types of students to experience the benefits of an IB education.

Davey and Fuller's definition of a hybrid qualification includes the following access opportunities which the CP should be able to provide for students:

- Full access to HE
- Access to all HE institutions
- Access to bachelor degrees
- Access to all subjects (not only to cognate subjects)
- Full access to the labour market
- Access to the skilled labour market (beyond or within an occupational field)
- Access to professional body memberships
- Licence to practise
- Wage return on qualification

- Social partner recognition (e.g. trade unions, chambers)
- Access to next level of training
- Access to work-based career pathways

This checklist provides a useful perspective on what such a hybrid qualification may be able to offer CP graduates. The demographic of students will invariably change now that CP is open to a wider range of post-16 institutions, and so the checklist should be helpful in guiding the future positioning of the programme by the IB. The CP market demand will dictate its ultimate success, but if it sets out to achieve the aims stated in 2012:

- *providing a more inclusive provision for students aged 16–19*
- *responding to the IB's mission statement and extending the influence of international education*
- *filling a gap in international education*
- *reducing the "academic versus vocational" divide* (IB, 2012)

then a new group of CP students and new institutions should gain access to an IB education for the first time.

Hybrid qualifications present an obvious additional complexity in gaining recognition. Because the IB is not responsible for the recognition of the career-related studies that are largely, but not exclusively, the design and often the pride of a nation, it has little quality control over this aspect of recognition or equivalence. Institutions (HE and employers) accepting graduates will need to grapple with and understand more than one type of qualification with this programme.

A different perspective on recognition will need to be thought through. Students may not opt for HE, some will want to go straight to the work-place, or join corporate entities as high-level apprentices or set up their own businesses as young entrepreneurs. A broader view of recognition that engages the corporate world, industry and accrediting partners should begin to emerge.

Lesson learned from the recognition journey of the DP

There are a number of important considerations the IB, as an organisation, would have taken into account when embarking upon the development of a new programme. The questions that new CP school/colleges will ask are largely the same as those pioneer schools that embarked upon the recognition journey during the six year trial of the DP back in the 1970s: will the qualification be recognised in the home country of the (international) student and will there be a credible higher education pathway?

The added career-related dimension of the CP will also need to answer the questions: 'Will the CP be recognised by employers and industry partners as a credible qualification for the world of work? Will the challenges for the CP in becoming recognised be greater or less compared with the recognition and adoption of the DP? Are the challenges for the CP even greater because it is a hybrid qualification that brings together a nationally recognised qualification with known international components (DP courses), plus a new and unique IB developed CP core?'

Since the first DP examinations were held in 1970, the progress towards DP recognition has been steady. Alec Peterson, the first Director General of the IB, recounted that by March, 1969 every university in the UK had been contacted and asked to accept DP students. "All but seven had accepted" (Peterson, 2003, p 69). But there was an on-going difficulty with the recognition of international qualifications by national systems; this difficulty still exists today to some degree. Peterson argued for the following solution:

"What was needed, therefore, was simply the recognition of the IB (DP) as a secondary school-leaving certificate, after which the mobile student could compete in the normal university selection on equal terms with those who had attended national schools at home" (Peterson, 2003, p 69).

By the end of 1973, a six year period, 20 countries had agreed a general, and others partial, recognition for the DP (or equivalence to the secondary leaving certificate) on this basis. DP students were already attending 175 different universities in 25 countries (Peterson, 2003, p 71). By 2012 the DP was recognised in 87 countries and was offered in 141 countries (IB, 2012). In the nearly 50 years of the existence of the DP, the programme is now offered in 143 countries and DP students apply to 3,300 HE institutions each year (IB, 2016). A remarkable achievement considering recognition is not achieved at government level with all of those countries. An equal focus on HE institutions and governments gave the DP secure foundations at its launch.

The CP is at the very early stages of recognition worldwide. By comparison, the pioneering DP was described at being in its 'infancy' until 1983 (Bunnell, 2011), and only became accredited in the UK in 2000 in what Bunnell went on to describe as the 'coming of age years' (Bunnell, 2011, p 128). At this stage the DP had been in existence for over 30 years and had significant currency with HE institutions around the world.

Ian Hill, former Deputy Director General of the IB, lists several 'helpful milestones' that supported the DP in gaining good recognition (Hill, 2010):

- The support of influential stakeholders in the formative years (e.g Lord Mountbatten)

- The support of high ranking universities in UK, US and Canada to accept DP students

- The inclusion of the IB in the appendix of the European Commission's agreement of the mobility of workers through their recognised qualifications (Council of Europe, 1999)

- EU mobility agreements such as the Lisbon agreement and the development of the Bologna process

- DP accreditation by QCA/Ofqual in England in 2000

- Growth and adoption by well regarded schools

- Government announcements in support of the IB. For example, Prime Minister Tony Blair supporting the DP in state schools in 2006

Hill's milestone list is a useful reference point for the CP that may give insight to support current recognition work.

Is it realistic to think that this pathway of recognition and support for the DP should lay good foundations for the sibling qualification, the CP? With the advancement in wider transnational bodies involved in global recognition practices, referenced previously, and since the launch of the DP in 1968, one would expect that the CP would have an easier passage.

Recognising the very clear differences between the two programmes and comparing the DP and CP journeys, it may seem like the DP had a better start. The DP gained full or partial recognition in 20 countries within its first five years, compared with a handful for the CP since its launch to DP schools in 2012. Statements of full or partial recognition at government level for the CP have been established in England, Spain and the Netherlands (IB, 2016) although this is not fully documented on the IB website. HE statistics showed that 175 universities accepted DP students in the first five years and the data from IB in 2014 listed 114 HE institutions accepting CP as an entry qualification. Progress in HE institution recognition therefore looks favourable should CP graduates wish to choose an HE route, but perhaps a governmental approach is still worthy of further investment to help secure the value of the programme and provide state or public funding. At the time of writing, the CP is offered in 21 countries with significant uptake in the US and UK.

Referring to the helpful DP recognition milestones (Hill, 2012) and learning from the past may prove to be useful for looking to the future for CP, particularly with regard to recognition of qualifications in countries that require more regulation and recognition efforts. Recognition in terms of equivalence with secondary leaving certification still needs to happen in certain countries so that no student is disadvantaged by opting to choose the CP pathway, nor prevented from receiving available funding, nor excluded from HE in the country in which they are living.

The positioning of the the CP and its impact on recognition

Positioning an IB programme at its launch and in its subsequent years plays an important role in how the programme is acknowledged and accepted internally within IB, and recognised externally by wider stakeholders. This section will consider how the CP was first offered, marketed and positioned at its launch, and how it is positioned today.

The CP was first piloted in 2007 and continued in its pilot stage until 2010. DP schools across the world were invited to join the pilot, and a diverse group of schools in both private and public education became willing volunteers. The initial response by IB schools showed a commitment to adding a professional and career-related offer to the existing pathways for post-16 IB students. In 2012 the CP was officially launched and offered to all existing DP schools.

Offering the CP to DP schools only in the first phase of the launch may have been regarded by some as giving an unrealistic picture of future uptake. Given the challenging nature of the full DP as an academic qualification, what types of school would be interested in the CP? Since the launch period, it has been demonstrated that a career-related programme of international education is of considerable interest to a wide span of institutions: US community colleges; UK selective grammar schools; long-standing international schools; private international boarding schools. Through a unique and successful partnership pilot in the county of Kent, UK (see chapters 9 and 10), a cluster of non-DP schools was able to introduce the programme, representing a much closer match to the schools likely to take on the CP once it was offered more widely. However, the early CP adopters were those schools that already had interaction with, or knowledge of, an IB education through the worldwide reputation of the DP.

The following extracts are taken from the IB websites in April 2012, when the programme was launched, and in July 2016. Several changes have occurred since its launch in terms of programme name change, and alterations to the programme structure, content and aims. It might be perceived that the CP had a somewhat clumsy, tentative beginning, with unexpected setbacks and changes. Perceptions matter enormously in the introduction of a new programme, and a clear message about the nature of the programme and its intent was critical for a fourth IB programme to be embraced.

The two descriptions of the CP between 2012 and 2016 show some marked differences. The four aims of the CP in 2012 reveal a broader agenda relating to access and inclusion; its positioning is less defined in the current text used to describe its aims. The access agenda may not be such a high priority now.

The IB website described the CP (then named the IBCC) in the following terms:

Programme overview and aims in 2012

"The IBCC incorporates the educational principles, vision and learner profile of the IB into a unique offering that specifically addresses the needs of students who wish to engage in career-related education. The IBCC encourages these students to benefit from elements of an IB education through a selection of two or more Diploma Programme courses in addition to a unique IBCC core, comprised of an

approaches to learning (ATL) course, a reflective project, language development and community and service. It has four aims:

- *providing a more inclusive provision for students aged 16-19*
- *responding to the IB's mission statement and extending the influence of international education*
- *filling the gap in international education*
- *reducing the academic versus vocational divide*" (IB, 2012)

Programme overview in 2016

The International Baccalaureate Career-related Programme (CP) is a framework of international education that incorporates the vision and educational principles of the IB into a unique programme specifically developed for students who wish to engage in career-related learning. The CP's flexible educational framework allows schools to meet the needs, backgrounds and contexts of students. CP students engage with a rigorous study programme that genuinely interests them while gaining transferable and lifelong skills.

The CP helps students to prepare for effective participation in life, fostering attitudes and habits of mind that allow them to become lifelong learners and to get involved in learning that develops their capacity and will to make a positive difference. The programme aids schools' retention of students, promotes development of skills, and encourages students to take responsibility for their own actions, encouraging high levels of self-esteem through meaningful achievements. A key feature of the CP is that it provides flexibility to allow for local differences. Each school creates its own distinctive version of the CP to meet the needs, backgrounds and contexts of its students

Clarity about what the CP is and whom it is intended to reach are critical for those bodies wishing to recognise and accredit it. Ensuring there is enough conviction about the programme as a relevant and highly valued offer will affect its capacity to be recognised by all stakeholders.

Government and non-governmental recognition

Good government recognition of the CP has been achieved in England in so much as the regulator Ofqual (The Office of Qualifications and Examinations Regulation) has granted HE credit for not only the existing DP courses but for elements of the CP core (Language Development; Personal and Professional Skills; Service Learning; the Reflective Project). Funding was also secured for its implementation in the state school system. More recently the CP has appeared in new government accountability measures in England, which means it is listed as an approved qualification (DfE, 2015).

Several attempts have been made to secure recognition and equivalence in the United Arab Emirates (UAE), but this is still not confirmed at a UAE federal level, meaning that the CP is only currently offered in Dubai. Difficulties recognising the career-related element that schools may choose from a different provider means some programme offers will have partial but not full accreditation. Perhaps greater collaboration with providers needs to happen to consolidate support and provide joint efforts towards recognition practices.

Favourable indications of recognition support have come from other governments including advocacy statements for the CP in Spain and funding agreements for state international schools in the Netherlands, plus support from Dutch technical universities. Within the Netherlands the CP has now been added to the NUFFIC website, the register of approved qualifications, as a level 4 qualification (NUFFIC, 2016).

Funding agreements are amongst the strongest elements of recognition that can support the mobility of students and their future success, and they feature as a strong recognition indicator in many countries, in particular in the US where CP growth is the most prolific.

Another form of non-governmental recognition and advocacy may be worth additional focus. On visiting UNESCO colleagues in 2014 and presenting them with an overview of the programme, the technical and vocational UNESCO staff welcomed its addition and suggested the IB was well placed to be a forerunner in career-related education as it does not have its origins in any national vocational system. Perhaps some recognition from UNESCO would be the best type of global validation any international programme could gain so that the CP can be seen as a real contender to become a leader in its field.

Recognition by higher education institutions

The availability of destination and recognition data at this stage of the CP's development is limited, but several important reports and a university list produced by the IB in 2014 provide some emerging trends relating to destinations and the HE response to the CP.

Research commissioned by IB with the Warwick Institute for Employment Research (IER, 2016) focused on the CP global graduates in 2014, and in particular the student experiences, post-secondary school destinations and their outcomes. The survey was completed by 339 graduates from seven countries, the majority of whom came from the UK and US; one employer and eight HE institutions were also surveyed. 53% of the students went on to enrol in HE institutions; 75% felt that the CP had prepared them well for HE. Two thirds of the 53% enrolled in HE felt the career-related study and Reflective Project were helpful to them.

Of those students surveyed, 8% were in employment connected to their career-related study; 21% were in casual employment; 5% were engaged in other activities including military training or extended holidays; three students were engaged with apprenticeships or training; 10% of the surveyed students indicated they had experienced unemployment after finishing the CP.

The evidence, thus far, from the first cohorts of CP students graduating at the end of their two-year study shows that students are securing pathways into HE more than they are into the world of work. This may not be surprising when the focus for selecting CP schools has been predominantly on existing DP schools.

In 2014 the IB provided a list of 114 global HE institutions that were accepting CP students or the CP qualification. In the US, 48 HE institutions had accepted CP graduates and 39 in the UK. A further 27 HE institutions in the UK recognise the CP as an entrance requirement. In Europe, 14 universities were listed as recognising the CP as an entry requirement. Ofqual recognition in England essentially means the qualification is listed as an accepted entry qualification to university, so all institutions are obliged to accept it as an entry qualification.

The University Admissions Report 2015, commissioned by the ACS International Schools group (based in the UK and Qatar), IBSCA (IB Schools and Colleges Association, based in the UK) and the IB, interviewed 80 UK admissions officers and 20 from the US. The report documented that 65% of the universities' admissions officers had heard about the CP. The effort to date with recognition of the CP by HE institutions shows good progress.

The wording used to describe how HE institutions are accepting CP graduates needs careful consideration as the DP and CP will no doubt be compared. The statements below from the IB highlight a tentative approach from the organisation, not necessarily the best reflection of the research and evidence now available:

"Universities and further/higher education institutions are likely to value the CP for a number of reasons."

Compared with

"The International Baccalaureate Diploma Programme is recognised and respected by the world's leading universities"

(IB, 2016)

With several cohorts of students having entered and finished HE since the first pilots in 2007, together with data that has been gathered in recently commissioned research, the messaging around the CP on the IB website could reflect greater conviction and cite examples of actual destinations in order to give confidence to future participating schools.

Recognition by employers

The CP is now open to all post-16 institutions worldwide, offering the first programme of international education focusing on professional skills and career-related pathways. Recognition at employer level may be of greater importance than the current focus on HE. If the CP is recognised as a full secondary school leaving certificate, it will open up more pathways to the access routes described by Davey and Fuller. Accelerating and securing advocacy and recognition by high profile employers in given professional pathways would be a key to CP success. Working in close partnerships with leading employers to secure graduate pathways, and direct or sponsored routes to employment, would also help steer the nature of recognition towards a career-related focus if the CP is setting out to do what it claims it wants to do in its own words -

"The International Baccalaureate Career-related Programme prepares students for the world of work, as well as developing a student's personal qualities. By doing so it leads students down a personally chosen pathway towards further/ higher education, apprenticeships or work" (IB, 2016).

We may see a change of focus in years to come in what is meant by recognition and how it is managed by IB. At the time of writing the research and views of employers available are too limited to comment on fully in this chapter, but a response from one of the pioneer CP schools emphasises the need to place more effort on recognition by industry:

"Our school has offered the DP and CP as our sole Sixth Form provision since 2012, with our numbers increasing year on year and with students and parents recognising these programmes as a clear pathway. With the majority of our students progressing to university with relative ease, and this number increasing year on year, one might presume recognition (of the programme) is successfully growing. However where recognition is key for the CP is in industry. If it is truly to live up to its mission statement, it must be understood for the unique opportunity it provides young people to progress in the world of work – by the world of work. This is a more difficult and less familiar territory for many Sixth Form providers."

Rebecca Pickard, CP Coordinator

Dane Court Grammar School, Kent, UK

Recognition through collaboration with partner organisations

Since its launch in 2012, the IB has developed formal partnerships with a number of organisations in order to collaborate with compatible partners providing career-related studies and qualifications. The four organisations below recognise the value in the CP to the extent that they have signed formal agreements with the IB:

- **Pearson**, for BTEC qualifications. Pearson is a global, multi-sector organisation

- **IFS School of Finance**, a UK based financial services organisation

- **Project Lead The Way (PLTW)**, which offers science, technology, engineering and mathematics (STEM) programmes in US schools

- **National Academies Foundation**, which provides education in finance, hospitality, engineering and healthcare in the US.

By way of its design, the CP is the embodiment of a partnership between two education providers and it will be essential to have a clear message from the IB regarding the direction of partnerships going forward. The number of partnerships has not grown since 2012 for what may be valid reasons, but there is no clear direction or invitation for others to join and be welcomed on board. Perhaps signed agreements are not needed now, but a market place for schools and colleges to share who they have partnered with when designing such a hybrid programme would be more than relevant in an age of sharing and open source access to knowledge.

Strengthening recognition of the CP

It may prove helpful to the success of the CP for a broader view of recognition to be developed and articulated by the IB. The IB could extend its public definition of recognition to encompass the needs of both internal and external stakeholders. Recognition needs to go beyond the focus on HE and university/college entrance. If harnessed effectively, employers and corporate partners will become aware of, and accept and advocate on behalf of the CP. Developing a recognition strategy to reflect this will be important in the next phase of the CP's development.

Comparing the journey of CP with that of the DP, and considering that it was not until the DP was over 20 years into its existence that it appeared in the English qualifications registry, it is clear that the CP is significantly aided by early government recognition and HE acceptance in those countries where recognition is a bridge to educational mobility. Funding in US state colleges, and partnerships with organisations like Project Lead The Way, resulted in a promising rate of adoption of the CP in US state schools. The IB has the influence, technology and capability to provide outreach, so it may be thought that the task will be an easier one in gaining recognition for CP. But the challenges for CP are greater than they first seem. The fact that there are four IB programmes provides more challenge and greater leverage of resources for the IB than at the time the DP was launched in 1968. Also the CP, as a hybrid qualification, relies upon partnering with organisations that offer qualifications in career-related studies; this partnering also requires its own journey of recognition. Leveraging governments and international bodies like UNESCO would serve the CP well as it did in the early days of DP recognition.

Recognition is best achieved if embraced by the whole community. Recognition starts at post-16 schools and colleges, and institutions that recognise the importance of this will be the greatest advocates of all for the CP. Leveraging CP success stories will be of enormous benefit to recognition of the programme.

Joint efforts for recognition would also be advantageous in mobilising the power of many, so gaining advocacy statements from high profile corporate entities would hugely benefit global recognition of the CP.

I would also argue that more strategic partnerships need to be forged by the IB as the CP begins to develop clear professional routes. Since the start of the pilot phase few new partnerships have been agreed. Finally, public visibility of recognition successes requires a greater profile. To demonstrate a positive picture of success more emphasis may need to be given to making this information readily accessible.

The CP has achieved a number of successes in the field of recognition, despite some tentative positioning by IB. However, the IB will need to harness the momentum created by its advocates in this next phase of CP growth as the programme moves from a closed group of DP schools to a wide-ranging new group of schools and colleges whose students will benefit from an IB education for the first time. As the CP grows it needs to be bold in its confidence, and strong in negotiating recognition with governments and a wider range of stakeholders, in order to celebrate the enormous potential of this highly marketable and important educational programme.

References

Bates, R. (2011): *Schooling Internationally: Globalisation, Internationalisation and the Future for International Schools.* London, UK: Routledge.

Bunnell (2011): *The International Baccalaureate: Its growth and complexity of challenges.* In R Bates (ed) *Schooling Internationally:* Globalisation, Internalisation and the Future for International Schools. London, UK: Routledge.

Blair, T. (2006): Keynote address at Specialist Schools and Academies Trust (SSAT) conference.

Burgen, S. and Hunt, E. S. (2008): *Developing attitudes to recognition: substantial differences in an age of globalization.* Council of Europe.

Davey, G. and Fuller, A. (July 2011): *Best of Both Worlds or falling between two stools: the case of hybrid qualifications in England.* Southampton, UK: Southampton University.

Department for Education (2015): 16-19 accountability headline measures. Available at: www.gov.uk/government/uploads/system/uploads/attachment_data/file/482225/16_to_19_accountability_headline_measures_technical_guide.pdf#page65

European Commission (1999): The Bologna Declaration. Available at: ec.europa.eu/education/higher-education/doc1290_en.htm

NUFFIC, (2016) www.epnuffic.nl/en/diploma-recognition/overviews-foreign-diplomas/overview-diplomas-international-baccalaureate/?searchterm=international%20baccalaureate

Hill, I. (2010): *The International Baccalaureate: Pioneering in Education.* The International Schools Journal Compendium Vol 1. Woodbridge, Suffolk: John Catt Educational.

International Baccalaureate: (2012) International Baccalaureate website. www.ibo.org

International Baccalaureate: (2016) International Baccalaureate website. www.ibo.org

International Baccalaureate (2015): *The University Admissions Report 2015.*

Ofqual (2012): Register of Regulated Qualifications. Available at: register.ofqual.gov.uk/

Oxford Dictionary Online (2016): Oxford, UK: Oxford University Press.

Peterson, A. (2003): *Schools Across Frontiers: The Story of the International Baccalaureate and The United World Colleges 2nd edition.* Chicago, Illinois: Open Court.

Walker, G. (2011): *The Changing Face of International Education.* Cardiff, International Baccalaureate.

Warwick Institute of Employment Research (2016): *The International Baccalaureate Career-related Programme (CP): Students' Experiences, Post-Secondary Destinations and Outcomes.*

Chapter 3

Developing lifelong learners: an overview of the Personal and Professional Skills component of the Career-related Programme

Chantell Wyten

Introduction

Sitting in the IB global office in The Hague in the summer of 2014 I knew we were onto something. Despite the inviting weather outside and the call of a nearby beach and Dutch summer vibes, the synergy in the meeting room was unmistakable. Our team hit a reflection point that afternoon. Collectively stopping to review the many planning documents in front of us and high level diagrams mapped on the 'war room' white-board walls, one thing was abundantly clear: we had pieced together an ambitious and flexible brave new course that truly honed in on the relevance and positioning of career-related learning, for individuals and educational institutions alike.

One of the unique and fundamental aspects of working with the IB, as many teachers will know, is the respect the organisation has for practitioners' 'chalk-face' experiences and ideas in informing curriculum advancement. The small team that was invited to be part of the Career-related Programme (CP) Approaches to Learning (ATL) review meeting represented a breadth of IB schools: new, established, private and state. Reviewing the, then, ATL course was an opportunity to capitalise on our varied experiences and present challenges to the CP thought-leaders at the time, so that ATL could evolve from a course that had a bedrock of skills-based content to a signature and fleshed out component of the core of the CP (ATL, Service Learning, Language Development and the Reflective Project) that would be seen as being meaningful and detailed as its IB Diploma Programme (DP) core counterparts (Theory of Knowledge; Creativity, Activity and Service; Extended Essay). The planned outcome was to replace the CP's ATL with a course with more career-related alignment.

To say we were fired up and ambitious for the future of the IB's newest programme was an understatement. Just meeting CP colleagues felt like an immense privilege, like being reunited with family members with whom you shared a parallel history. In the review meeting, discussions of context and approach demonstrated a unified commitment to advancing CP practice and teaching tools, particularly for this component of the core, as a vital course that could be fashioned to the needs of learners in any international setting.

Early on in this curriculum review meeting we had an informal group conversation about the seminal TED talk by Ken Robinson: 'Do schools kill creativity?' (Robinson, 2006) on which we shared a common view: a hierarchy of subjects is something that should be questioned, in all contexts. As Robinson pointed out, intelligence is diverse and dynamic, children's potential unlimited and the challenge of education is always to prepare young people for futures we cannot predict. As seasoned educators we had all experienced individual students who had been stigmatised for talents and interests that did not appear traditionally 'functional', but who went on to be successful on the basis of these talents. ATL, for all of us, represented a welcome opportunity to address this anachronism and an opportunity to draw both teachers and students to the IB mission through a course that could go some way to resolving a common fear that all teachers have: am I focusing on the right things?

What has now become the CP's Personal and Professional Skills (PPS) course is an absolute commitment, on behalf of the IB and its teachers, to offering curriculum that fosters diversity, embraces divergent approaches to career-related learning and encourages teachers to understand the learner's unique learning story; to individualise rather than impose a 'one size fits all' journey. In completing the ATL/PPS review, the team felt the new PPS guidance was more purposeful, stimulating and capable of invigorating the deep commitment of teachers to create transformative conditions for their students.

An overview of the Personal and Professional Skills course and its place in the core of the CP

The CP was originally developed to meet the rising global demand for a framework of international education that would bridge the academic-vocational divide, respond to the IB's mission statement, and provide greater access to an IB education. Launched in 2012, the CP underwent a full curriculum review between 2014 and 2015 to absorb the lessons from its pilot phase. During this period each component of the CP core was reviewed and revised to build on the conceptual and interdisciplinary approaches from the IB Middle Years Programme (MYP) and align with the DP core where appropriate.

The CP core is at the heart of the programme, contextualising the DP subjects and the school selected career-related studies, drawing all aspects of the framework together. The four components of the CP core are designed to develop the characteristics and attributes described in the IB Learner Profile. Comparisons to the DP core can be made, though the programmes are unique and distinct. The core of each programme unifies the student experience, both as learners engaged in an IB programme of learning and as part of the international learning community. There is something profound about having global solidarity with other IB learners through a parallel core experience.

Central to the CP is the belief that teachers involved in its provision should be aware of career-related trends, as well as the transferable skills students need to acquire to be successful in life beyond the qualification, in order to address the most pertinent issues for their students. The voice of the learner should be at the forefront of the learning process, not the voice of the teacher. The teacher is the guide and facilitator in the process of student learning. This belief is what guides the PPS course.

PPS has evolved to a 90 hour, internally-assessed course, structured around five themes that represent the key areas of student development in terms of attitudes, skills and strategies for now and in the future:

- personal development
- intercultural understanding
- effective communication
- thinking processes
- applied ethics.

PPS is an explicitly career-related element of the entire CP framework designed for students to explore issues and ideas from their career-related studies and apply new understandings to personal and professional situations. Emphasis is placed on the dynamic links between all kinds and ways of learning throughout the CP journey. Each school is able to design and develop its own bespoke PPS course so that it is of-the-moment and addresses the needs of those particular students.

Though by design it is essential for PPS courses to be ubiquitous and progressive, the following basic tenets are the desired outcomes for CP students; I have adapted them from an unpublished early document on the CP in order to explain in more detail its learning outcomes:

- **Develop a sense of social awareness, community involvement and social action**
  The student should be able to recognise a need in the community and most importantly be prepared to act to make a difference.

- **Recognise issues of equity, justice and responsibility**
  It is important that the student is able to look beyond himself or herself and recognise issues of inequity and injustice both locally and internationally.

- **Increase their awareness of their own strengths and areas for growth**
  The student is able to see herself or himself as an individual with various skills and abilities, some more developed than others, and understand that they can make choices about how to move forward.

- **Undertake new challenges**
  A new challenge may be an unfamiliar activity, or an extension to an existing one.

- **Plan and initiate activities**
  This can be shown in activities that are part of larger projects, for example service learning activities in the local community, as well as small student-led activities.

- **Work collaboratively with others**
  Collaboration can be shown in many different activities, such as working in teams and helping the local community resolve a problem.

- **Show perseverance and commitment**
  At minimum, this implies attending regularly, completing assigned tasks and accepting a share of the responsibility for dealing with problems that arise.

- **Engage with issues of global importance**
  The student may be involved in international projects, but at minimum, the student has developed a sense of international mindedness.

- **Consider the ethical implications of their actions**
  Ethical issues arise throughout the core activities, and the student must show that ethical principles have played a role in decision-making.

- **Develop new skills**
  New skills may be shown in activities and tasks the student has not previously undertaken, or in increased expertise in an established area.

At this point it is worth noting the explicit links that the CP, especially the PPS component, has with other IB programmes. Whilst the CP is a high quality programme in its own right, and appropriate for delivery in schools that do not already offer any IB programmes, there is specific alignment and articulation with the other IB programmes. From the MYP foundations of creative, critical and reflective thinking, the PPS course enables learners to diversify their MYP experiences by providing opportunities for teachers and students to enhance the connections between subject knowledge, personal skills and the real world. For example, whilst the theme of personal development is prescribed in PPS, the medium or topics for inquiry and learning are for schools to decide. Therefore links to prior learning, like the MYP concepts, may prove a fertile starting point upon which learners can build their new learning.

Ultimately, through engagement with all the themes of the PPS course, students are able to take the IB mission further by beginning to explore how their future career and lifelong learning ambitions may shape, and be shaped, by personally, locally or globally significant ideas and issues. This unique approach in PPS has been well received by teachers and there has been affirmation that the MYP 'lives-on' through the course, whilst retaining the freedom and trust older learners require to explore their own aptitudes. As one teacher and consultant recently put it: "How do you get kids to be innovative? You let them. You get out of their way."

PPS has also helped to define the relationship between the cores of the CP and the DP, central to both programme models. The DP core has gained the respect of leading universities around the world for broadening students' educational experience. The CP core takes a similarly interdisciplinary approach to the complex and controversial challenges its learners encounter. The constructivist learning that take place in PPS develops the attributes of the IB Learner Profile, and additional attributes for 16 – 19 year olds, including responsibility, perseverance, resilience and self-esteem. It is worth noting that unlike the Approaches to Teaching and Approaches to Learning in the DP, which are addressed from within the DP courses, PPS is purposefully structured as a stand-alone course. In this sense PPS has drawn comparisons with the Theory of Knowledge course (TOK), advocating critical thinking and an open-minded approach. A student, from a school offering both the CP and the DP, reflects: "From what I understand, in the CP and DP we are looking at our beliefs and assumptions, but in the CP we look at the impact of these in the real world and our future lives more".

Why Personal and Professional Skills works

One of Carl Rogers' contributions to educational psychology was what he described as 'significant learning' which rests upon the 'realness' of the relationship between facilitator and the learner. According to Rogers, the facilitator should 'endeavour to organise and make easily available the widest possible range of resources for learning' and 'regard himself as a flexible resource to be utilised by the group' (Rogers, 1969). PPS curriculum design enacts this lesson in both curriculum and assessment design. The IB has charged schools with developing their own method of assessing learning outcomes and the progress of their students in PPS. As such, schools are able to emphasise local or even individual priorities through the balance of themes and the assessment methods they choose. Emphasis is placed on the cycles of genuine feedback that promote behaviours and skills integral to life after the CP, which also help to create a culture of valuing reflective practice, not only in the classroom, but across all aspects of the programme. Put simply, PPS is a microcosm of what many communities value as adaptive, meaningful education.

In various contexts recurrent benefits of PPS have emerged:

- Raised aspirations in students who have gained greater awareness of their skill sets, as well as what motivates them as individuals and contributors to communities

- Better understanding of appropriate progression routes through a commitment to understanding personal motivation and current trends in education, training and employment

- Lasting community involvement with individuals and groups that has evolved from genuine mutual interests and the desire to work collaboratively

- Enthusiastic engagement with a curriculum that prioritises real world learning and skill development, and that teachers feel comfortable in tailoring to their students' needs.

UNESCO's recent Incheon Declaration has given clear pedagogical direction for all nations: "Education 2030 will ensure that all individuals acquire a solid foundation of knowledge, develop creative and critical thinking and collaborative skills, and build curiosity, courage and resilience" (UNESCO, 2015). The CP addresses this declaration, providing a flexible and malleable framework for schools to respond to their local needs and develop students' capacities, as outlined in the declaration, to make a positive difference through fostering attitudes and the habits of mind needed for personal success.

Beyond the five learning outcomes of PPS that set down adaptable, future-focused learning goals, there are also supportive suggested topics, subtopics, discussion questions and related activities. Additional support for teachers through IB professional development encourages teachers to introduce other contextually appropriate topics and partner with students through learning tasks characterised by exploration, connectedness and real-world purpose. The following strategies are recommended:

- Varying types and lengths of activities

- Seeking opportunities to integrate learning outcomes or themes

- Conducting medium to long term or whole-class projects

- Employing teaching strategies that spark interest and further questions

- Taking learning beyond the classroom.

Compared to the other components of the core, PPS has lent itself to numerous examples of creative and flexible approaches, as evidenced in CP literature and forums, which exemplify future directions for education. One-off PPS lessons evolving into whole community projects or students taking charge of their learning environment are commonly cited experiences in the course. A CP coordinator from a school in Kenya describes how a poster-making lesson, based on the theme of thinking processes, initiated a class discussion that led to the class supporting a nearby primary school to gain access to drinking water, and to refurbishing the students' toilet facilities. Clearly, the significance of incidental learning that PPS enables cannot be overestimated.

There is anecdotal evidence from IB workshops that teachers value the topics detailed in the PPS guide. Many have considered the complementary use of the principles of universal design for learning (CAST, 2012), which aim to optimise teaching based on scientific insights into how humans learn, alongside the PPS course in order to better meet the needs of most students. The new guidance on PPS (IB, 2015) represents a holistic approach to learning that promotes learner autonomy and self-actualisation. It is clear that teachers have capitalised on this when we hear repeated themes in their learning journeys. For example, it is common practice for PPS teachers to spend planning time on consideration of methods and materials that allow for multiple means of student engagement and expression, seeking support and clarification from various sources of IB guidance, for example forums and workshops. Recently a workshop leader commented on her on-line PPS participants: "They certainly don't look for shortcuts and I never had to prompt conversations to keep them generating ideas or discussion!"

An additional clear message in interviews and feedback from PPS teachers is that the course has increased their confidence to challenge ability-based thinking and practices. Removing the negative messages of grading and hierarchy allows the emphasis to be on each student's experience and development. The IB is amassing evidence on the increased motivation both teachers and students feel because of the unique approach to learning and assessment that PPS promotes: highlighting each individual as important, equal and multi-skilled. All this provides us with a timely reminder that 'education is not the filling of a pail, but the lighting of a fire' (attributed to WB Yeats, but hotly debated).

Currently new sets of teacher support materials are being developed for PPS, promoting a range of appropriate methodologies and a continued focus on transparent, collaborative reflection which will help drive school self-evaluation and planning cycles. There has been some discussion about the value of a PPS textbook. While textbooks still have a place, it is acknowledged that they are static and expensive learning-support tools. Increasingly, teachers use social media, virtual learning technologies and resources they produce themselves to support learning in current and interesting ways. The IB seeks to promote and showcase a range of the good practice which is already taking place in PPS; for example a US county which enables students to connect virtually with peers from nine other similar but distanced schools on a PPS learning platform.

When viewed in the larger picture, with its relationship to the other elements of the CP framework, students have been overwhelmingly positive about the PPS course. A student who featured in an IB video publication (IB, 2013), off-camera, summarised the value of PPS succinctly: "Before the CP I was not really sure what I was doing with my life. I certainly felt school didn't have the answers for me, lesson by lesson it was all so 'paint by numbers'. In PPS we have a choice of what and how we learn; that has inspired me to look into so many areas of life without judgement, just open-eyed interest. I know myself better now people have stopped telling me what I should know."

Challenges for the future

As with all feedback from skilled and talented IB teachers, comments can be insightful, provocative and contradictory. The clear message that the IB has received from educators about PPS is that they want the course to continue developing along the same lines. They like it very much! Though in part a wonderful affirmation of the direction PPS has pursued, it is a statement that poses challenges as the organisation continues to be aware of the professional teaching capabilities that must be developed for new curriculum and pedagogies to be effective. The CP necessitates teachers and students becoming excellent lifelong learners, individually and collectively. Nowhere is this truer than in PPS. This statement generates multiple challenges which the IB seeks to address.

The IB will not rest on the praise PPS has been given. Encouraging innovation, systematic effort, insight and compassion, not just in what goes on in the classroom but also in the ways the IB works and relates to schools and educators, is at the forefront of the plan ahead. New means of measuring and valuing personal and professional success are urgently needed to provide students, teachers, parents and leaders with a clear picture of what career-related learning really means in practice, and how it can positively affect the futures of young people.

The IB will also continue to promote teaching strategies which shift the focus from covering content to the processes of learning, developing students' capacity to lead their own learning and to do things with their learning. There is a real need to ensure that all areas of the CP, but especially the DP courses, have relevance to students' career goals. Pervasive digital access has led us to appreciate that whilst breadth of knowledge is important, teachers and schools should not be viewed as mediums of delivery. Learning should be focused on helping students to master the process of learning, thereby enabling them to navigate and manipulate the rapidly evolving tools and resources in their world.

A further area for development is ethical education. An early comment on the former ATL course was the need to make ethics a more defined part of the course, both in support of the Reflective Project and to make explicit ways of dealing with ethical scenarios in business and the wider world. Ethical education takes place in all components of the CP and the core is no exception. The core provides a major opportunity for ethical education, encompassing principles, attitudes and codes of behaviour. While there are ethical principles embodied in the IB mission statement and Learner Profile, the emphasis in the core is on helping students to develop their own identities and beliefs. In developing content for this PPS theme it was understood that various ethical issues would arise in the course of core activities, and may be experienced as challenges to individual students' ideas, instinctive responses or ways of behaving (for example, towards other people). In the context of PPS, teachers have a specific responsibility to help students think, feel and act their way through ethical issues. I would suggest that there are real opportunities to explore ethics further in future iterations of the PPS curriculum, through an emphasis on social justice, complexity and personal responsibility.

Conclusion

John Dewey stated: "Many young people leave school with the attitude of wanting and expecting to be told, rather than with the attitude of realising that they must look into things, must inquire and must examine" (ed. Boydston, 2008). Decades on, this attitude is still a pervading issue for educators, governments and businesses alike. The world beyond school, with its digital lures and overhanging threats of future unemployment, pulls young people away from any learning perceived as irrelevant and, equally, creates pressure for educators to balance the teaching of content and skills with adaptive personalised approaches. The PPS course attempts to address these issues. Despite standardised assessments stigmatising failure and creating hierarchies of subjects, there is a clear need for a counterbalance in education which reflects real-life approaches to the assessment of personal performance.

It can be summarised that the value of the PPS component of the CP core lies not only in the career-specific skills it harnesses and connects back to the classroom, but in the inbuilt flexibility it gives communities to feed curiosity and experiment with new learning environments. PPS actively encourages that which is outdated or irrelevant to be called into question. Researching what qualifications and skills may be valued in the future continues to be an important priority in determining the direction of PPS growth.

PPS balances the necessary elements of thoughtful curriculum design with a desire to guide teachers in a way that goes beyond elaborate platforms or pedagogical trends. Schools as we know them may not exist in the near future. There is a possibility of no school campuses, current qualifications having little or no value, and the confluence of technology with education valuing real world experience and portfolios over knowledge and qualifications. Certainly no knowledge or curriculum is secure. So far the CP has been successful in adapting to educational shifts and needs, continuously seeking to learn from educators and learners in developing new approaches and building learning communities. PPS stands as testimony to the CP's proud history of growth, its potential for today and as a component of a programme that is also truly flexible and forward-facing in its intent.

References

Boydston, J.A. (ed.) (2008): *The Later Works of John Dewey*, 1925-1953. Vol. 9: Essays, Reviews, Miscellany, and A Common Faith. Carbondale, Illinois: South Illinois University Press.

CAST (2012): *National Center On Universal Design for Learning.* Available at: www.udlcenter.org/

International Baccalaureate Organization (2013): *IB Career-related Programme.* Available at: vimeo.com/79667818

International Baccalaureate (2015): *Personal and professional skills guide.* Geneva, Switzerland: International Baccalaureate Organization.

Provenzano, N. (2012): What's the future of education? Teachers respond. Available at: blog.ed.ted.com/2016/02/12/whats-the-future-of-education-teachers-respond/

Rogers, C. R. (1969): *Freedom to learn.* Columbus, Ohio: Merrill.

Robinson, K. (2006): *Sir Ken Robinson: do schools kill creativity?* Available at: www.temoa.info/node/1595

UNESCO (2015): *Incheon declaration: education 2030 – towards inclusive and equitable quality education and lifelong learning for all.* Washington, DC: World Bank Group.

Chapter 4

Why Service Learning matters in the Career-related Programme

Cathryn Berger Kaye

Can you imagine a high school academic programme that includes opportunities for students to:

...analyse workplace protocols for a nonprofit organisation and make recommendations for ways to attract a younger workforce?

...participate in the redesign of a park space to meet the needs of families with young children and people who want to exercise?

...assist a local food bank in a marketing plan for better outreach toward a sustainable supply of food, appropriate for the population being served?

...find ways to minimise food waste at school, home and in a local restaurant?

If these kinds of opportunities were among the offerings at your school, would that entice a high level of student engagement? We all know that showing up is not enough. Schools today must aspire to create meaning and establish purpose for students so that they arrive at school eagerly and actively pursue their education. How can this be done?

Schools today recognise the high level of value that comes from providing connections with the community to augment learning, assist with application of knowledge and skills, strengthen positive dispositions, and facilitate the transition from school to career and college. Fortunately, this can happen in high schools; in fact it is a core aspect of the IB Career-related Programme (CP) by design, and achieved partly through Service Learning.

With high quality Service Learning, the CP offers students opportunities to connect academic content and their career-related studies with purposeful action. Clearly, students (like their teachers) want school to be worthwhile, to have meaning and purpose, and to open doors to a vibrant future. School is a place for curiosity that provokes ongoing questioning and a desire to learn beyond the classroom and examinations. For today's youth, the confines of a classroom may restrict this exploration and discovery. Service Learning, as a pedagogy, has been called the fourth wall of a classroom that opens up to the world. This is why it is an ideal pedagogy for the CP, one of the aims of which is for students "to gain a deeper understanding of themselves, their community and society" (IB, 2015b).

Service Learning in the CP

In the context of the CP, Service Learning is the development and application of knowledge and skills towards meeting an identified and authentic community need. Students undertake service experiences often related to topics studied in their Diploma Programme (DP) courses, the CP core or their career-related study, utilising skills, understandings and values developed in these components of the CP. The process of learning through service enables students to make links between their school or work-based studies and their service experiences.

In the CP guide (IB, 2015a), Service Learning is noted as "a core component of the International Baccalaureate Career-related Programme", alongside the other three elements of the CP core: Language Development, Personal and Professional Skills, and the Reflective Project. These four CP core components are discrete elements, but are also integrated with each other and with the DP courses and career-related study that make up the three parts of the CP. The CP thus attaches value and importance to the integration of Service Learning. It also implies that learning through service is deserving, as a pedagogical concept, of time and effort to both understand what it is, and to develop clarity on how to weave it into classroom pedagogy and practice. In addition, this mandate implies the expectation that administrators, teachers, and students will know their roles and responsibilities to bring this concept to life. This idea extends to parents and family members who are also essential in offering support for the students; family support can be the difference between an indifferent and an engaged student. To be effective, Service Learning cannot be separated from other critical elements in a school, or relegated for one person to understand and implement. Such separation or relegation would be contrary to the idea of a 'core component'. The good news is that understanding Service Learning can advance the school's priorities and improve approaches to teaching and learning.

What is also significant is how Service Learning is described in the IB's guide to the CP: "The process of service learning provides opportunities for students to understand their capacity to make a meaningful contribution to their community and society" (IB, 2015a). Take note of the word 'process', a word that implies there is a series of engagements that add up to the total experience. Fortunately, Service Learning is a well-developed, research-based process that makes good sense to educators. As teachers come to know this process, articulated in five stages – investigation, preparation, action, reflection, and demonstration – they see how it aligns with best teaching practices and supports the integration of a dynamic and engaging approach to teaching and learning. The process of Service Learning, when done well, adds a welcome dimension for teachers that strengthens their professional expertise.

The CP Service Learning Guide also articulates the impressive benefits of Service Learning for students, and how it aligns with other valued aspects of the IB programme:

"Service learning provides opportunities for students to understand their capacity to make a meaningful contribution to their community and society. Through service learning, students develop and apply academic knowledge, personal skills and social skills in real-life situations involving decision-making, problem-solving, initiative, responsibility and accountability for their actions. The purpose is for students to contribute to society by improving the lives of people or assisting the environment or animals." (IB, 2015a, p 6).

These attributes, from decision-making to accountability, are best learned by being in a situation where they are forthcoming through experience. They are learned from the inside out. To understand decision-making requires us to be in a situation where we make a decision that extends beyond a case study or the hypothetical to something that is real. There is quite a difference when students make a decision on a question posed on a test or during a simulation about hunger, and when they make a decision standing in a food bank where others are depending on the response. Suddenly, response-ability (hyphen intended) and accountability have meaning. Immersed in experience, students can apply prior learning and extend their learning with new ways to think and question: Why is there a shortage of fresh produce? What is generational poverty? Who is at greatest risk in our community? How can my choices and actions contribute to the well-being of others? The unique nature of the CP allows students to combine their academic studies with career-related studies and with Service Learning, a three-pronged approach that can provide relevant, powerful and immersive experiences.

The aims of Service Learning

Service Learning in the CP has clearly articulated aims to assist educators to align the process with student benefits and achievements. Through engaging in Service Learning, the foremost aims are for students to:

- develop and apply knowledge and skills towards meeting an authentic community need
- develop as leaders who take initiative, solve problems and work collaboratively with others
- enjoy the experiences of both learning and service
- develop a sense of caring about, and a responsibility for, others
- gain a deeper understanding of themselves, their community and society through meaningful student reflection
- enhance and strengthen their experience with the existing school curriculum

(IB, 2015a, page 6)

In the next section on the purpose and process of Service Learning, each of these aims will become clearer regarding how this can be achieved.

Consider though that I have called these the 'foremost aims' since these are noted in the CP Service Learning Guide. However, with well thought-out Service Learning in the CP, you will likely see an additional range of benefits for students. For example:

- a questioning mind developed through curiosity about real world contexts

- clearer understanding about how culture and history intersect

- making connections that might otherwise be missed

- an expanded point of view by being exposed to diverse ways of thinking and being

- an appreciation for the contribution made by people in different careers, including non-profit organisations

- the ability to observe change over time with a recognition of ways to overcome obstacles

- clarity on how to build and sustain community partnerships

- knowledge of how local and global issues are interwoven

- replacing a personal emphasis on extrinsic rewards with the valuing of intrinsic rewards

- knowing that their learning, thinking, and actions matter.

What may be most exciting about Service Learning is all of the benefits cannot be predicted; there is an element of the unknown as students embark on a journey of discovery. So often we, as teachers, are expected to know what will happen, and be able to chart each outcome. With Service Learning the adults have to let go of some of the control in order for the student to have a real experience and to stretch enough to meet these aims. Rather than a learning environment shaped by the idea of controlling and managing youth, the more we – the adults – engage and inspire, the more the students will flourish.

Another, often overlooked, aim of Service Learning is to assist students in knowing a reliable method for addressing the challenges and opportunities that they will inevitably experience, whether in school, personally, or in the workplace. The Service Learning stages can be applied to diverse situations, providing students with lifelong skills and understanding for how to move forward with decision-making, gain deeper understanding of a situation, and meet change with a positive attitude.

Understanding the purpose and process of Service Learning

Service Learning moves the acquisition of skills and knowledge from the singular benefit of the student, most often noted with a grade of accomplishment, to engaging students in applying their abilities and knowledge toward a public purpose. The process necessitates a deliberate academic and service connection and includes students taking initiative, authenticating needs, developing reciprocal collaborations with community partners, and participating in meaningful reflection. Service Learning is not glorified community service, it is much more: it is an effective teaching methodology that, when done well, improves student engagement and the classroom experience for students and teachers.

A proven method of Service Learning follows these five stages (see Figure 1):

1. Investigation

Investigation includes an inventory of student interests, skills, talents, and social analysis. When we start with getting to know the students – understanding their interests, skills and talents – we can continually draw upon this knowledge and add to it over time. The students are thus more likely to be valued by the group, and to stay engaged. For example, when a group of students was planning a collaborative Service Learning project, they built upon their interest in music and their concern about people in the community living with HIV and AIDS. They decided to partner with a concert venue and a popular musician's performance, and set up information tables. When a student noticed a girl in the group was withdrawn, he remembered her interest in fashion. Suddenly he proposed the theme of the campaign to be "It's in fashion to know." The otherwise disengaged girl lit up, and immediately jumped in designing a poster that excited everyone.

Investigation also includes social analysis and gathering information about the community, both the assets and needs. If only the needs are examined, the students are employing a deficit model of community; looking at assets first acknowledges community values and strengths while building partnerships. For example, as students were working with a health care organisation to find out about community needs, they added questions to discover community assets and strengths. They found elders highly skilled in knowing the medicinal values of plants in the area. Through further interviews, they influenced the health care organisation to highlight local knowledge in their continued community work.

A preferred method of action research includes gathering information about assets and needs through the MISO method (Kaye, 2010): using Media, Interviews of experts, Surveys of varied populations, and Observation/personal experiences. Once learned, this MISO method augments research skills that can be applied in college and career situations. During investigation, students also consider how any local issue they discover can be understood in a global context. Similarly, if students aim to work from a global perspective, they look through a local lens to see its pertinence in their own backyard.

2. Preparation

When well done, investigation will raise further questions that need attention. Students are then propelled to continue to acquire academic content knowledge and apply knowledge and skills from their DP courses and their career-related study, as they deepen understanding, identify partners, organise a plan of action, clarify roles, build time-lines, and continue asking questions and developing skills. It is common for students to want to go immediately from investigation to action, but without the planning and preparation stage the action is less likely to be effective. By deepening their knowledge and augmenting skills, students become more sensitised and aware of the importance and complexity of the issues they are dealing with, and are more likely to develop the internal motivation to follow-through on their action since people (or animals, or the planet) are depending upon them. This stage also allows for the local-global connection to be further studied and understood.

Some students were at a Habitat for Humanity worksite assisting in the construction of a home alongside the family who would be living there. A family member approached the organisers and pleaded with them to stop the teens working. Perplexed, the organiser asked why. The response: "They have no idea how to hammer a nail! They are destroying the house!" Clearly, these students had skipped the preparation stage in their urgent rush to action! Many layers of preparation would have had mutual benefit for the students and the new homeowners.

3. Action

The action is planned with partners based on mutual understanding and perspectives, aiming for reciprocity of benefits. Students implement their plan in the form of one or more type of service: direct service, indirect service, advocacy service, or research service. As noted in the CP Service Learning Guide:

> "By engaging in different types of service within the CP, students accumulate different ways of knowing about their community and their potential for contributing to social change" (IB, 2015b, p 16).

- Direct service: Student interaction involves people, the environment or animals. For example, this can appear as one-on-one tutoring, developing a garden in partnership with refugees, or working in an animal shelter.

- Indirect service: Though students do not see the recipients of indirect service, they have verified that their actions will benefit the community or environment. For example, this can appear as redesigning a non-profit organisation's website, writing original picture books to teach a language, or nurturing tree seedlings for planting.

- Advocacy: Students speak on behalf of a cause or concern to promote action on an issue of public interest. For example, this may appear as initiating an awareness campaign on hunger, performing a play on replacing bullying with respect, or creating a video on sustainable water solutions.

- Research: Students collect information through varied sources, analyse data, and report on a topic of importance to influence policy or practice. For example, they may conduct environmental surveys to influence their school, contribute to a study of animal migration, compile effective means to reduce litter in public spaces, or conduct social research by interviewing people on topics such as homelessness, unemployment or isolation. [Author's note: Research service is different from the action research done during investigation; it derives from understanding that further research is the need and the research will be put to use, not just done for a grade.]

In the event that students decide to work on a global issue, it is quite important for them also to take local action within the same theme of service, otherwise service can be perceived as exotic or something we do from a distance. When service is local, students have more sustained time to deepen understanding, ask questions, develop relationships, and learn about the different roles and responsibilities that people take on when championing a cause or assisting the local community.

Examples of types of action:

- Direct service needs to be ongoing and sustained in order to be effective. When students sign up for a service opportunity, and get on a bus to go to a centre for children with special needs, for example, to play sports or lead an art activity, and have no investigation or preparation, the resulting action is often of minimal value and may lead to incorrect information about the children. There is rarely a reciprocal exchange in these situations. However, in a high school where students study special educational needs and related topics in several courses, or read a novel, or have conversations in science/psychology, they are more likely to design (assisted by conversations with the centre staff) appropriate activities that will have value and merit for the children, and stereotypes will be replaced with accurate information. Even one curricular connection can make a significant difference. Sustained and ongoing direct service will have greater impact and benefits for all involved.

- Indirect and advocacy service require careful investigation and preparation as much as direct service. For example, students had been studying about issues of school and community safety and were directed to make a poster about the issue and put it up in school. This resulted in over 40 posters which were largely ignored. This is not acceptable service. This is what I call service to tick a box: done! However, in another school, students verified a need for an educational campaign on community safety with a local organisation addressing this local issue. The students were asked to meet a real need: create a series of six posters to reach different target audiences, from young children to elders, and to assist with translation. They partnered with a public relations firm, and divided tasks. In groups, students took different approaches to learning and pooled their knowledge. This included reading about advertising strategies, assessing other posters designed for these populations, and actually running focus groups. The six resulting posters, created through a collaborative effort, were well-valued and all were used in the community.

- Research service: During investigation, a social studies class was using a human rights website for their studies when they realised there was limited updated information on the otherwise excellent website. By contacting the organisation they discovered a need: staffing changes and lack of interns meant the organisation was behind in website development. The teacher adapted the upcoming research paper assignment to focus on assisting this organisation. This meant that students had to be rigorous with sources and they worked much more concertedly because their information would be reviewed and published.

4. Reflection

Reflection is ongoing and occurs intermittently during all stages of Service Learning as a considered summation of thoughts and feelings regarding essential questions and varied experiences to inform content knowledge, increase self-awareness, and assist in ongoing planning. This is a critical engagement that also assists students to consider their developing and evolving ethics, the impact of their choices, and how they may consider what this experience tells them about their everyday actions. However, we all know that reflection is sometimes perceived as a burden to students, an imposition and a set of expected responses to, again, tick off the 'done' box. This especially occurs when reflection is overly prescribed, timed, evaluated, and limited in how it is done.

Reflection in the Service Learning process, rather than being required, should be inspired—inspired by significant moments that deserve time and attention because something has happened that matters, or an idea has been provoked or challenged. There are a multitude of reasons for reflection but inspired reflection is more likely to happen when the adults involved open up the possibilities, and model and accept diverse ways of reflecting. Consider how much treasured music, art, and writings have been created in moments of reflection.

The CP Service Learning Guide states:

"During service learning, the form of reflection must take into account student choice. When overly prescribed, students may perceive the act of reflection as a requirement to fulfil another's expectations. Students may then aim to complete "a reflection" quickly since the value is unrealized. By contrast, the student who understands the purpose and process of reflection would choose the appropriate moment, select the method and decide on the amount of time needed. With this greater sense of autonomy and responsibility, the student may be encouraged to be more honest, forthcoming and expressive, and develop insights including those related to the learning outcomes. The ultimate intention is for students to be independently reflective and to enjoy the process and chosen method of reflection" (IB, 2015a, p 19).

A key purpose of engaging students in reflection is not to have them complete meaningless, hollow assignments, but to enable them to become reflective people so that they will choose to become reflective on their own. With this in mind, the CP aims to invigorate the reflective experience, and hopes this more meaningful approach to reflection finds its way into all parts of the CP programme.

For example, a teacher had been giving students reflection tasks, such as to "submit five reflections by Friday." He found them repeatedly sterile and very prescriptive, as if they were all telling each other what to write. Then he changed the language: "Be on the lookout for a significant moment as you take part in your service experience." He led a brief conversation about what makes a moment significant, leading to a list of thoughtful ideas, such as: "when I get really interested in what's happening", "I had a gut level reaction", "I burst out laughing with my elder buddy", or "when I thought about what I wanted to do next time". Each student had more detail in what they wrote about as they isolated moments that mattered. Another teacher, who likes photography, invited the students to take a picture "that says it all, no caption needed", and this led to a truly engaged reflective conversation where everyone participated for the first time.

5. Demonstration

Students capture the total experience including what has been learned, the process of the learning, and the service or contribution accomplished, and they share that experience with an audience. Telling their story may integrate technology and often educates while informing others. The same idea of letting students draw upon their interests, skills and talents and areas for growth should guide what and how the students pull together the important moments and learnings to share with others. Do they create a short video that shows the evolution of their work and process, from investigation through preparation, action, and ongoing reflection? Perhaps compile a scrapbook that is constructed during the diverse experiences that add up to Service Learning? Art, music, photography, presentations, videos, articles, calendars, magic shows—there have been students who have done each of these to communicate what they learned during each stage of Service Learning, the community connections made, and the issues understood from local and global perspectives.

Figure 1: The Service Learning process (© 2014 wwwCBKassociates.com)

When does Service Learning happen in the CP?

A critical question to consider is when does Service Learning take place? If Service Learning is only done by students independently, they may approach this with uncertainty about the concept and process. The IB states that: "The process of service learning is best when understood and organised as an ongoing experience occurring with regularity throughout the duration of the student's CP" (IB, 2015 a).

There are four responses to the 'when' question in the CP.

1. When administrators, coordinators and teachers understand and value the process of learning through service, it can be applied to a myriad of components within the CP, particularly the career-related study. This is optimum. If, for example, in a career-related study the teacher employs Service Learning to deepen understanding about the content (investigation) and then identifies a current need that magnifies students' understanding of this content, Service Learning has relevance. For example, a career-related studies teacher was exploring sports management with his students. During one unit on events management in a sports tournament, as a class task, the teacher asked his class to identify how they could make use of their understanding and skills to host a sports tournament for a deserving community group. The class undertook a study of the various community groups in their area then, after some research on each, reached out and contacted a community group responsible for hosting beach clean-ups. The students proposed an awareness

campaign for a bi-monthly beach clean-up through a sports event to be held on the beach. The students duly organised the sports tournament, advertised the event in conjunction with the community group and held a successful sports day. By doing so, they also raised awareness of the bi-monthly beach clean-up, resulting in stronger volunteer attendance as a result. What occurred with the beach clean-ups, however, is that the students legitimately got tired of cleaning up the same beaches! They then began to analyse the litter and search for the source. For example, an over-abundance of straws (very dangerous for sea creatures when they get in the ocean) led students to recommend a no-straw policy to the local food kiosks, along with signage to explain why. With Service Learning, students aim to get to the causative factors of societal issues and thus gain the capacity to make lasting change.

Additional brief examples are provided in the CP Service Learning Guide:

- Students learn about an event in recent history and as a result, collect local stories from elders to contribute to the library and historical archive. Students develop both inquiry and documentation skills.

- In a literature class, students create and perform a contemporary version of a play for elementary children. This increases the students' understanding of the original text while developing their collaboration, writing and communication skills.

- In a mathematics class, students assist in designing a community parking lot to maximise the numbers of parking spaces while ensuring adequate spaces for accessible parking for disabled people.

- For a science class, students identify a location for a rainwater garden then install and maintain it as a model for the local community.

When teachers resist Service Learning, thinking it is a distraction from the academic syllabus, clearly they misunderstand the intention and the process. With knowledge of learning through service as pedagogy, teachers find it can be the impetus for deeper understanding and interdisciplinary connections, and for more engaged students. In their academic studies, students are likely to shift from 'I have to', to 'I want to', and this is a considerable change.

Equally important, when Service Learning is integrated into the CP, particularly in the skills-focused career-related study, and the process made transparent (i.e., now we are investigating, now we are preparing), students come to know explicitly and understand the five stages of the Service Learning process. If they experience the process in this explicit manner more than once within the CP they will know this process well.

2. Then, we come to the response to the question: "When is Service Learning?" as stated in IB regulations: During the Service Learning experience, going through the five stages of Service Learning over a period of 18 months, and documenting this in the Service Learning portfolio. If students approach this concept with

no prior experience with learning through service, it's easy to understand how they would be overwhelmed and see this as a huge challenge. However, if they are building their understanding of the purpose and process of Service Learning through all components of the CP, they are more likely to get it and also to find a connection with a topic or community issue they care about.

3. A third response to "When is Service Learning?" is when students, by choice, engage in an additional group service project. When students understand the five stages that guide the process, they are more confident and capable of applying this methodology as they work with their peers and/or the community in reciprocal partnerships.

4. The fourth response: anytime students engage in community action.

Outcomes for Service Learning

When the IB's approach to Service Learning in the CP is understood and followed, students readily meet the five learning outcomes:

- Identify own strengths and develop areas for growth

- Demonstrate participation with Service Learning experiences

- Demonstrate the skills and recognize the benefits of working collaboratively

- Demonstrate engagement with issues of global significance

- Recognize and consider the ethics of choices and actions (IB, 2015a, p 7)

With Service Learning we develop students who self-identify as change agents. Of course change is a constant. However, we are referencing the intentional change implied in the quote by artist Andy Warhol: "They always say time changes things, but you actually have to change them yourself" (Warhol,1977). Instigated change occurs with awareness, collaboration, problem-solving, momentum, perseverance, and resilience.

It seems we are currently experiencing a global groundswell of service and civic engagement. The issues we face as a planet have risen to a level that calls us all to action. We can be engaged in learning about and addressing critical interrelated issues—hunger, potable water, climate change, population migration, loss of habitat, illiteracy, gun violence, war—while contributing to the betterment of ourselves and others. Students who become cognisant of the issues and have problem-solving abilities to address them find an advanced imperative for learning that extends well beyond grades. When students lack the skills to address these relevant issues and topics, then all educators need to take notice and provide what is needed to transform youth into advocates for the social well-being of our environment, our communities, and this planet that we share. Providing the requisite skills and knowledge to do this vital work in local communities and the larger world adds purpose to the process of education, and of Service Learning, and prepares students for this century of change.

A key aspect of the CP is to generate students who are able to transfer what they learn and experience in these formative years into transferable life-long skills and knowledge, supported by a healthy disposition. Words fill classrooms and books and computer screens; we can dialogue, write papers, and make suppositions about possibilities, yet, when we take words and transform them into ideas, and these ideas then transform into action, what are we capable of? Bringing learning to life through using what we study in class to assist students to gain skills and confidence, writing informative brochures about preventing heart disease, alerting communities to environmental toxicities, growing fresh vegetables in areas designated as "food deserts," or guiding students to see and engage with their community in authentic and meaningful ways—can this be what education is really about?

In *Now You See It*, Cathy N. Davidson writes: "The world is full of problems to solve that cost little except imagination, relevant learning, and careful guidance by a teacher with the wisdom to not control every outcome or to think that the best way to measure is by keeping each kid on the same page of the same book at the same time" (Davidson, 2012).

With Service Learning, ideas become a reality; excitement becomes palpable; contributions are significant. Students discover who they are as personal interests, talents, and skills, and self-identified areas for growth connect with the academic content and skills. Service creates purpose for learning. Students, and exceptional educators who engage them, prove to be valued contributors for our collective well-being, now and in the future.

Service Learning has changed many lives, including mine. I have seen the world with new eyes, and been transformed by people through their stories and their dedication to community. I am encouraged by younger generations who know that we face astounding challenges and see learning through service as a process that will be viable for the children they will nurture into stewards for our collective future.

References

Davidson, C. (2012): *Now You See It: How Technology and Brain Science Will Transform Schools and Business for the 21st Century.* New York City, New York: Penguin Books.

International Baccalaureate (2015a): *Service Learning Guide.* The Hague, Netherlands: International Baccalaureate.

International Baccalaureate (2015b): *Career-related Programme: From principles into practice.* The Hague, Netherlands: International Baccalaureate.

Kaye, C. B. (2010): *Complete Guide to Service Learning: Proven, Practical Ways to Engage Students in Civic Responsibility, Academic Curriculum, & Social Action.* Minneapolis, Minnesota: Free Spirit Publishing.

Warhol, A. (1977): *The Philosophy of Andy Warhol (From A to B and Back Again).* New York City, New York: Mariner Books.

Chapter 5

The Reflective Project: a journey into the world of ethics in the Career-related programme

Patrick Daneau

What is the link between the use of human embryos in the USA, the rights of foreign workers in Dubai, the damages caused by the tourist industry in Mauritius and the behaviour of British soccer players off the football pitch? They are all ethical issues analysed by IB Career-related Programme (CP) students as part of their Reflective Project. These sorts of ethical issues are at the heart of the CP and are the focus of the students' Reflective Projects.

This chapter has three parts: firstly, a brief description of the context of my involvement in the CP; secondly, a consideration of the nature of the Reflective Project; thirdly, a discussion of the universal nature of ethics and how the ethical issues which are at the core of the Reflective Project open candidates' eyes to challenging situations that arise in their immediate environment and foster international mindedness.

The context

I have been teaching for 25 years at Collège Garneau, a French medium college located a few kilometres from the historic district of Quebec City, Canada. I have a philosophy background, which is why I was asked to join the IB Diploma Programme (DP) at the college as a Theory of Knowledge (TOK) teacher. I still teach this DP component. In 2006, my college was invited by the IB to be part of the pilot that led a few years later to the launch of the CP, along with Oulun Lyseon Lukio, a school in Finland.

The reason why these two schools were approached is interesting. This goes beyond the fact that they are IB World Schools; after all, there are thousands of IB World Schools around the world. So why these specific institutions? It was mainly because they were located within national education systems that have a strong emphasis on, and provide considerable support for, vocational or career-related studies; therefore these schools were able to contribute their long experience and commitment to the development of a new career-related offering for the IB.

In Quebec the vocational students study alongside those in the pre-university programmes; they are on the same campus and follow four compulsory courses together: French literature, English as a second language, Philosophy, and Health and Physical Education. That means that a future doctor and a future police officer or a future computer programmer are in the same class. They do the same assessments and they have the same number of classroom hours. For instance, in my Philosophy class (non-IB), when I read a student's essay I do not differentiate in any way between the vocational or career-related focus of some students and the university preparation focus of other students. I am confident that both groups of students are able to reach the level of abstraction specific to this particular age group.

As an experienced TOK teacher, I was asked to participate in the development of the CP Reflective Project and the Personal and Professional Skills (PPS) course. I have since taught the PPS course and supervised many Reflective Projects. In 2010, I was asked by the IB to take charge of the global assessment of the Reflective Project. For more than eight years, I have received on my doorstep Reflective Projects from all over the world.

What do we do with them? We moderate them. Basically, we determine if the candidates' results, given by their teachers, match with the IB criteria. So when a school sends for moderation some Reflective Projects, we have to check if the marks are appropriate. Were the supervisors too generous? Were they too harsh? Whatever the situation, we must give marks that correspond to the candidates' level. By doing this, we ensure that the results are fair and equivalent all around the world.

The nature of the Reflective Project

The IB defines the Reflective Project in the following way:

"The reflective project is an in-depth body of work produced over an extended period and submitted in year two of the Career-related Programme. Through the reflective project, students identify, analyse, discuss and evaluate an ethical dilemma associated with an issue from their career-related studies. This work encourages students to engage in personal inquiry, intellectual discovery, creativity, action and reflection, and to develop strong thinking, research and communication skills" (IB, 2015, p 6).

Unlike the DP that is designed and prescribed by the IB, the CP is unique in letting each school choose the career-related studies most suited to local conditions and the needs of their students. What is the IB contribution? In addition to making available the full range of DP courses, from which students choose a minimum of two, the IB has shaped the core of the CP, composed of four parts: Personal and Professional Skills course; Service Learning; a Language Development component; and the Reflective Project.

What is the nature of the Reflective Project? First, it is expected that students devote at least 50 hours to the project. Apart from the two DP courses, the Reflective Project is the only component of the CP core that is assessed by the IB, and can be seen as the culmination of the two years of study and experience in the CP.

Candidates can present their Reflective Project in one of two ways: a 3,000 word essay, or a shorter, written essay of 1,500 words accompanied by an additional format – a seven-minute short film; a recorded spoken presentation of seven minutes; an interview recorded on audio/video; or a short play or a photo essay using up to 15 annotated images.

Whatever format the candidate chooses, analysis of an ethical issue must be at the heart of the Reflective Project. An ethical issue is an issue where there is an opposition between moral concepts, conflicting opinions or different approaches to a problem. In our human world, behaviours, laws and social practices depend on the criteria by which we estimate them to be valuable and right. These criteria are our moral values. They direct our lives, justify our choices and stipulate how we must act. But people may not agree on what is valuable and right and this can trigger a conflict or a discussion about what is right or wrong and morally acceptable or not. Ethical issues revolve around these opposing views, and the analysis of them, hopefully, leads to solutions. This is why it is usually said that the study of ethics is reflective: it interrogates and evaluates moral dilemmas that happen in contexts such as personal and family lives, workplaces, local or global communities. In other words, the adjective ethical refers to any debate that involves a moral dilemma. It is these dilemmas that should provide the focus for the Reflective Project.

The Reflective Project is a demanding piece of work. In the early years of the development of the CP there were many educators who had concerns about the capacity of students who are more career-focused to write and present a rigorous, subtle and truly reflective piece of work. Do CP students have the ability to write 3,000 words? Are they able to explore an ethical issue with sufficient rigour? Is the Reflective Project really appropriate for them? But those concerns quickly disappeared when the the first cohort of Reflective Projects were submitted to the IB. It soon became clear that CP students do have the capacity to reflect on their studies, and their future work, and were able to write effectively.

Of course there are challenges with the Reflective Project. Some CP candidates inevitably struggle with the ethical issue, the main problem being that instead of writing an analytical and reflective paper, they write descriptively. Although descriptive projects can be interesting, they do not fully fit the requirements of the Reflective Project. The problem is that purely descriptive projects invariably lead to a single answer or an explanation of why an ethical situation has arisen; these projects simply describe a social phenomenon or situation. Interrogative projects, on the other hand, provide a discussion and debate on differing points of view related to an issue that has an ethical or moral dimension. The IB has published a *Reflective Project Student Guide* (IB, 2014) with the aim of helping students avoid the confusion between descriptive and reflective projects, and teaching them how to develop a research question that will lead to an interrogative project not a descriptive one.

CP students have produced some outstanding Reflective Projects. Below are the titles of some successful projects that clearly demonstrate that students understand what an ethical issue is and are able to produce an in-depth body of work:

- Should minors with currently incurable diseases have the final decision on undergoing somatic gene therapy clinical trials?
- Should shark-culling continue off the coast of Western Australia?
- Is the use of broad data sharing in genomic research ethical?
- Should unpaid internships be considered unethical?
- Should international constraints be placed on images of women used by the advertising industry?
- Is it ethical to use sexual appeal in marketing?
- Music's copyright: Is it right to use parts of others' work in your own work?
- Should education be free?
- Is it ethical for pharmaceutical companies to profit from developing drugs that have been tested on animals?
- Is it ethically right for British travel companies to market high risk package holidays to young people?
- Should social networking sites be banned?

These titles gives us a window on the challenging realm of ethics that 18 year-old CP students are tackling with enthusiasm, commitment and skill.

Journeys into the world of ethics

There is something fascinating and unique about the CP: it asks young students who are focused on and motivated by a career-related approach to education to reflect on an ethical issue. This requirement is rare in national education systems. Engagement with ethical issues provides a valuable educational experience for CP students, opening their eyes to challenging situations that arise in their immediate environment, leading them to consider the global implications of such situations and, ultimately, fostering international mindedness.Two examples follow.

A first example comes from the IB examination session of May, 2013. I received from a British school the following Reflective Project: *Is the UK's rubbish another nation's treasure?* At first glance, the work appeared to me off-track because it seemed to lead to a descriptive project. But this was not the case. The author was a young man studying computer programming and his career-related study was in computer technology. He was quite sensitive to the number of electronic devices owned by his friends and relatives. He conducted some research into the issue and realised that the possession of these devices in the UK creates human and environmental problems in other parts of the world. In his research he discovered the reality of the lives of the workers in Democratic Republic of Congo (DRC) who have to deal with all the toxic elements coming from electronic devices recycled in the UK and sent to Africa. Diseases and poisoning are the daily lot of the men, women and children who work with these toxic elements. In addition, the extraction of and trade in coltan – a chemical compound that is present in all cell phones and laptops – in the DRC is linked to the civil war in that country.

The student concluded that British consumers have a moral responsibility toward the Congolese workers, which led him to these two ethical issues:

- Should there be more regulation in the UK regarding the possession of electronic devices, knowing it would reduce the profit for British businesses?

- Should wealthy countries stop exporting toxic materials to developing countries, even though many families in those countries make their livelihood from the recycling of these hazardous substances?

These ethical issues arose from the student's DP course and his career-related study and were impressively analysed. The beauty of the project was that it began with a local observation that drove the candidate to a broader investigation of a global problem and deeply ethical issue.

A second example is of a CP student on Collège Garneau's Police studies programme who noticed, during his training courses at the police stations of Quebec city, that there was debate about the wearing of visible religious signs from immigrant policemen. He also observed the complexity of the new urban reality: immigrants settling in the city, thereby transforming the town and the relationship between police and the citizens. That was a shock for him. After a presentation in class of a the relevant political and philosophical arguments regarding the appropriate balance between individual liberties and the public good, he decided to ask this very socially relevant question: *Is it acceptable for policemen to wear visible religious signs?*

The student looked at the different responses to this question in the US, France, the UK and in Australia. Needless to say, this question is complex and what works in one country might not work in another. His journey led him to multiple ethical sub-questions:

- Given that religion might be very important for a person, is the wearing of religious signs at work an inalienable right?

- Knowing that a policeman on duty represents the state, should police authority forbid the wearing of articles of faith?

Once again, the questions arose during the student's career-related study. They started from a local observation, and his career-related experiences drove him to consider and reflect on broader, global viewpoints, resulting in a thoughtful, analytical Reflective Project. Such a process is a contribution to the development of international mindedness and illustrative of the nature and intent of the CP.

Conclusion

The examples above illustrate the relevance and the value of the Reflective Project. Not only does it open candidates' eyes to issues that surround them, but it can help them to develop a global perspective on these issues. It is also likely, given the intensity of the experience of producing a Reflective Project, that the skills and attitudes the students develop during the process will follow them during their entire life.

As a final thought from a Reflective Project moderator and educator, the assessment of the Reflective Projects is extremely rewarding. I appreciate the variety of topics, the less academic nature of the process of producing the Reflective Project and, above all, the cultural diversity of the final products. The ethical issues have given me glimpses into individual societies. I have learned about immigration in Dubai, work behaviour in Finland, the tourist environment in Mauritius, food habits in Hong Kong, community policing in Canada, wildlife in the United Kingdom and ecological issues in the Unites States. All of this makes the Reflective Project and the CP unique and rewarding.

References

International Baccalaureate (2014): *Reflective Project Student Guide.* The Hague, Netherlands: International Baccalaureate.

International Baccalaureate (2015): *Overview of the Career-related Programme.* The Hague, Netherlands: International Baccalaureate.

Chapter 6

Language Development in the Career-related Programme: putting it into practice

Alexandra Juniper, Sara Woodcock, Ramona Dietrich, Mike Worth and Catheryn Phipps-Orive

Introduction

Learning a language has always been at the heart of an IB education.

Many students live in a monolingual and mono-cultural environment and because of this may become "culture-bound individuals who tend to make premature and inappropriate value judgements about their as well as others' characteristics" (Genc and Bada, 2005, p75). This type of environment can lead to a form of ethnocentrism that promotes a misplaced sense of pride, limits personal growth and contributes to a suspicion of people who are different. Learning a language and developing intercultural curriculum can help overcome the limitations of mono-cultural perspectives. In the Career-related Programme (CP) the IB specifically emphasises the importance of intercultural understanding and its role in developing caring, open-minded students who are preparing for the world of work, thus the inclusion of a Language Development (LD) component in the core of the programme that stresses intercultural understanding as well as language learning.

A successful intercultural curriculum will enable students to understand the meaning of culture and its relationship with language, to recognise the origins of their own cultural background and appreciate the similarities and differences of other cultures. The cultivation of intercultural understanding is part of the process of intercultural learning. It is not the acquisition of a particular area of knowledge, or the development of a particular skill, but rather the development of a range of skills and attitudes which can be called 'competence'. "Intercultural communicative competence is an attempt to raise students' awareness of their own culture and, in so doing, help them to interpret and understand other cultures" (Rose, 2003, p.4). Intercultural learning is, therefore, the process of knowing more about, and as a result, reaching a better understanding of, one's own culture and other cultures. "It is a dynamic developmental and ongoing process, which engages the learner cognitively, behaviourally and affectively" (Paige *et al*, 2000, p 2).

Language and culture are inextricably linked. Language is defined by a culture. In fact language can be said to be the medium of culture, as well as a determinant of culture. In other words, language is the expression of culture and, therefore, we cannot effectively learn and understand a second or additional language if we do not have an awareness of that culture, and how that culture relates to our own first language/culture. Learning another language and about another culture can allow students to enter a new, mysterious and exciting world.

The LD component is one of four compulsory components of the core of the CP, the others being Personal and Professional Skills, Service Learning and the Reflective Project. LD ensures that all students have access to and are exposed to a language programme that will develop their understanding of the wider world. The ability to communicate in more than one language is essential to the IB's concept of an international education, and LD, essentially, encourages students to improve their proficiency in a language other than their best or first language.

The aims of LD are to enable students to understand and use the language they have studied in context, to encourage an awareness and appreciation of the different perspectives of people from other cultures, to provide students with a basis for further study, work and leisure through the use of an additional language, and provide the opportunity for enjoyment, creativity and intellectual stimulation through knowledge of an additional language. LD is designed to accommodate all students, regardless of the level of linguistic proficiency they have when they begin the programme, and ensure they are exposed to a language that will further their knowledge and understanding of the wider world.

Students are expected to devote a minimum of 50 hours to LD over the two years of the CP, though schools are encouraged to provide a greater number of hours suitable to the students' aspirations where possible. The school is responsible for the ongoing assessment of the course, however, CP students must maintain and complete a language portfolio to document their learning activities and provide evidence of language engagement and development. This language portfolio is not assessed by the IB, but the IB may request a sample of portfolios.

As part of the integrated framework of the CP the provision of LD should, where possible, relate to the career-related studies of the students. This provides the student with opportunities to explore how language is used in everyday situations and how it can support career-related aspirations. The LD course can be based around a theme linked to the students' career-related studies, with an emphasis on the culture of the language, thus fostering an international perspective.

Each school can decide how best to deliver LD. The options include:

- a school-designed course
- an extension to a DP Language Acquisition (Group 2) course

- an external provider of language development

- an online language course

- a school-monitored, self-directed language study.

Whichever option is chosen, LD should be designed to develop students' linguistic abilities, and it should be challenging, enjoyable and relevant for the students.

In terms of choice of language, students have different starting points, goals and needs. They begin the CP with a range and variety of language learning experiences so the choice of what language to study is entirely up to the school and students. Schools should try to ensure that students study the language that is best suited to their background and needs, and the language that will provide them with an appropriate academic challenge. It is very important that the language studied is not the student's best language; their choice of language should provide a challenging educational experience and should have a clear purpose.

The remainder of this chapter consists of five stories told by teachers and coordinators about the ways LD can be organised, adapted and integrated in CP schools, both state-funded and private international schools. They are presented as examples and suggestions that illustrate the flexibility and the potential of the LD component in the CP to enrich students' lives and support their career-related ambitions. Hopefully, they will also provide some inspiration.

Language Development at Campus des Nations, International School of Geneva: catering for individual needs

Alexandra Juniper, CP and DP Coordinator

Campus des Nations is the smallest and youngest campus of the International School of Geneva (Ecolint). We have been running the CP since 2013 and our classes have been small, ranging from 9 to 16 graduates. The CP runs alongside the DP which has between 60 and 75 students. Our student body is very diverse with over 113 nationalities and 79 mother tongues and it is against this backdrop that we have created bespoke LD options for individual students.

As part of their CP, many of our students choose to take two languages within their DP courses; these will be English and French or English and Spanish. Luckily we are able to offer a range of different levels of DP courses in those languages. At the beginning of their LD course each student identifies which language they wish to develop and sets objectives for it. With their teacher the students identify the levels at which they are currently functioning for all of the different language skills. This satisfies the requirement for the CP's LD component. The students who do not wish to study two DP language courses have the option to join a DP class, but not to sit the final DP exams, and just develop their language skills against their own objectives which they have set with the language teachers. To satisfy the requirement for 50 hours of LD they attend classes during the first year of the CP for three hours per week. Some students, however, want a different challenge; this year we have a group of three students who have chosen to learn sign language with one of our Learning Support assistants and follow an online course with her for two hours per week. Finally if none of these options suit the students' interests or needs, they can choose to follow an online language course such as those offered by Rosetta Stone, or take a language through Ecolint's mother tongue programme.

As the CP is a relatively new programme we are continually evolving what we are doing and it is thanks to the flexibility of the CP, the willingness of the staff, and the nature of the LD component that our provision can be tailored to each student. Since one of selling points of the CP at Ecolint is flexibility, we didn't want to make any option compulsory, but rather find the right course for each student and then monitor it. This arrangement is, of course, time-consuming; many conversations have to happen at the beginning of term with students and staff to find the best option for each student. To facilitate the organisation of LD in the CP, our Personal and Professional Skills teacher has set up an effective system in Google Classroom to allow her to keep a watchful eye on the development of each student's language portfolio in their different LD options.

Language Development at Anglo European School, UK: supporting work experience

Sara Woodcock, CP Coordinator

The Anglo European School (AES) in Essex was the first state-funded school in the UK to offer the DP in 1977, and the CP in 2010. As a recognised centre for excellence in language learning, in many ways the LD component of the CP is a natural extension of teaching and learning at the school and has always been central to the CP offered at the AES.

The students at our school come from a wide range of linguistic backgrounds. The current cohort of CP students includes native speakers of French and Portuguese, and students who will have studied two modern foreign languages to GCSE level (taken at 15/16 years of age). But we also have students joining the CP in the Sixth Form who have not studied any additional or second languages at GCSE level. AES is committed to supporting multilingualism as fundamental to increasing intercultural understanding and international mindedness, and is equally committed to extending access to an IB education for students from a variety of cultural and linguistic backgrounds. The challenge is meeting the individual language development needs of each student.

We require all of our students in the Sixth Form to study additional languages at the highest level possible in order to achieve their maximum linguistic potential. Our commitment to language teaching and learning is a critical component of our Sixth Form provision and fully reflects our commitment to fostering understanding amongst all the members of the school's community. Language is an instrument for building strong foundations of identity, diversity and culture for our students, so the importance of learning through and about language and culture are central to the LD course in the CP.

Students in the CP are offered a variety of options which ensure that, no matter what their previous language learning experiences, their LD course is appropriate for the context of their career-related studies, and provides a challenging and meaningful educational experience. Students can undertake an extension to their DP Group 1 (Studies in Language and Literature) or Group 2 (Language Acquisition) language course through a school-designed CP LD course for a minimum of 50 hours. For this students have access to native-speaker language assistants with whom they work on a weekly basis to develop their communication skills, and to supplement and enhance the language acquisition of their timetabled language classes. Evidence of language engagement and development is provided in the student's language portfolio. Currently this is kept as a traditional folder but we are looking to produce an e-portfolio in the very near future.

Our CP students can choose from a wide range of languages on offer including DP Higher and Standard Level programmes in French, German, Spanish, Mandarin, Japanese, Russian or Italian, as well as IB DP *Ab Initio* (for beginners) courses in Spanish, Japanese, Mandarin and Italian. Additionally an A Level course is available in some of these languages or, alternatively, a selection of introductory language courses.

The LD course at AES aims to:

- Enhance our students' cognitive potential; support them in developing metalinguistic abilities; and teach them transferable skills in learning languages

- Teach students to respect and understand the cultures embodied in languages and the cultural identities of others

- Provide students with an ability to perceive the relationships that exist among languages and cultures.

Most of the students who have been at AES prior to studying the CP will have already participated in our comprehensive exchange programme in years 7 to 11, whereby students are given the opportunity to participate in a two-week study visit, staying with host families. CP students can take part in a similar programme staying with host families but with an additional challenge of a two-week work placement. This is organised in conjunction with one of our partner schools and means students will immerse themselves in the language and culture of the host country, stay with families and use language at home and in the workplace. Many of our CP students have taken up this opportunity, although for an *Ab Initio* student of Spanish, for example, it can be very challenging both linguistically and culturally after only a term and a half of learning Spanish! Students keep a diary of their reflections on their experience which will form part of their LD portfolio.

To conclude, here are the words of CP students reflecting on their work experience and their LD course:

"It really develops your communication skills, improving your confidence and your overall vocabulary, which will be invaluable in teamwork and interviews."

"I believe in myself more as I know I can cope in a completely different country speaking their language."

"You are able to learn about Italian culture in a way you couldn't by going on holiday."

"Although I was incredibly nervous about the exchange, I had an amazing two weeks and I am still in contact with my host family. My French improved more than I ever thought possible and I gained a friend too."

Language Development at Oeiras International School, Portugal: project-based learning

Ramona Dietrich, in charge of Language Development

Oeiras International School (OIS) is a day-school beautifully situated in a rural setting in a small village on the outskirts of Lisbon, Portugal. OIS is a relatively new school (this is our seventh school year) and offers the IB Middle Years Programme (MYP), the DP, and CP. Our student body consists of 33 nationalities and English is the language of instruction.

LD at OIS is one step on the student's path to success in the CP. Our approach to LD is quite straightforward: English and Portuguese are both mandatory in LD at OIS. As dictated by the Portuguese government, the English course of study is 240 hours over 2 years, and the Portuguese course of study is 180 hours over 2 years. Students are linguistically prepared for their work-placement in Portugal and for further opportunities, whether scholastic or career related. Students can add a third language if it suits their needs.

The LD framework is in parallel for English and Portuguese. In Year 1 of the programme students focus on our school. OIS is steeped in history: the main building which houses the administration, science, music and language classes is a 17th century manor house. This historic venue on 14 hectares complete with a chapel, a fountain, a garden, farm animals, bee hives, Celtic ruins, not to mention a phantom, offers rich topics for the students to explore and experience.

Year 2 of the programme focuses on the larger world. Students concentrate their learning on global issues and cultural diversity. This year, in one English collaborative assignment, students decided to produce a video to help combat racism. They have individual and collective pre-production, production and post-production tasks. They are making real-life connections as they use the skills that they are acquiring in their career-related studies. In Portuguese, students had an individual project where they had to create a travel brochure for a destination of their choice, taking the role of a travel agent. This task, under the topic of tourism, entailed research, planning and application of the graphic design skills in the conception of their advertisement piece.

This year we have added new projects which include a school catalogue and a magazine. The catalogue produced by the students is designed to showcase the school and the school community. Students are asked to categorise the members of the school (administration, staff, teachers, support, students, etc.), focus on some individuals by writing short biographies, and document how each contributes to the school community. Another project asks students to develop a luxury magazine which would satirise 17th century life.

One of the challenges we faced was how to increase student motivation for language learning in the CP. One strategy was to move from small, prescribed tasks to project-based learning, with the aim of developing capable and proficient learners. The new project designs are drawing on the professional skills that the students are learning in their career-related studies. In addition, students have become a part of the unit design process. They are actively involved in unit planning by offering suggestions for topics and products, participating in decision-making, establishing goals, setting timelines and sharing their knowledge. They also are engaged in peer assessment. Students have moved into a more pro-active role and it is working well; the outcome is greater student enthusiasm and significantly improved quality of work. Students now realise the value of their efforts and take ownership of their learning; they appreciate the importance of the process and the impact that their work has on others. As a consequence, the CP students take more pleasure and pride in their work.

Language Development at Greenfield Community School, Dubai: a key link in the CP

Mike Worth, CP Coordinator

The LD course is an important and exciting component of the CP and it can play a significant role in linking the elements of the CP core with other parts of the programme. The IB has a clear language policy across all its programmes which supports multilingualism as a fundamental part of increasing intercultural understanding and international-mindedness. The IB is also committed to extending access to an IB education for students from a variety of cultural and linguistic backgrounds.

In the initial days of planning the CP at Greenfield Community School, it was difficult to grasp exactly what was expected of the LD component. What was this new subject? Should it be delivered by a language teacher? Should it be a stand-alone subject or integrated? How could it link with the DP courses? How could it support the career-related studies with their specific technical languages? How could it be linked with the other areas of the core? But as the programme started to take shape, it became clear that the LD course had to be more than just a traditional language course. Developing the possibilities of integrating it with other components of the programme was key, and I could see the subject, as it was explained by the IB, had the flexibility to create these important links.

Being based in Dubai we started with the Arabic language as the CP students were mainly first language English speakers. Following a conversation with a Cultural Studies teacher I began to see the benefit of developing a language and a culture course to not only incorporate language learning, but to widen the content to involve aspects of our local culture to which many students were oblivious, even though they had lived in Dubai for some years! Visits to a mosque and also the Sheikh Mohammed Centre for Cultural Understanding significantly helped to increase students' awareness and understanding of the richness of the Arabic language and culture, the history and the people of Dubai. Many students at Greenfield are choosing now to stay in Dubai to study at university and even work here, so there were tangible benefits to including these cultural studies in the LD course. As the programme has progressed, the Arabic speaking students who have joined the programme have helped with the teaching and learning, creating a dynamic environment for language learning.

It is vital that the four components of the CP core are delivered, as intended, with as much integration as possible. As our Service Learning (SL) programme developed we introduced a trip to the International School of Moshi (ISM), Tanzania, to work on projects in the community. Our SL project was to help a local primary school build additional classrooms. Linking our LD course with the SL trip to Tanzania was a great opportunity, and so our students developed key language skills in Swahili, and some understanding of the culture of the the Maasai tribe, the local area of Moshi and the importance of the famous Mount Kilimanjaro. When our students arrived in Tanzania they were well prepared: they could greet the local children at the school, they sang a welcome song in Swahili, and had some understanding of local customs. The LD course added a significant dimension to the SL project.

As our CP continues to evolve our students have developed confidence in the use of a range of languages in a variety of contexts and with specific projects. We have taken on smaller projects in our local community to support ancillary staff at the school who come from the Philippines, India, Bangladesh and Sri Lanka. Students have cooked for and hosted a lunch of cultural foods, all linked with developing awareness of these cultures and learning the languages.

When planning a LD course, I would encourage schools to identify opportunities to link a language component to as many other elements of the CP as possible. A link with a local community is a good place to start as it builds awareness and cultural understanding, and an international trip can develop excellent cross-curricular links. The focus on cultural studies together with the development of the language is a very a positive way to approach LD and can help to build a strong and vibrant CP.

Language Development at Alameda International Jr/Sr High School, Lakewood, Colorado, USA: language learning for professional interaction

Catheryn Phipps-Orive, Language Development and language portfolio coordinator

The aim of our LD course within the CP is to blend language development seamlessly, but explicitly, into the career-related studies we offer to students for the express purpose of developing language as a necessary and applied, professional skill within a globally connected social world.

Implementing Language Development

Alameda, a state-funded school in Colorado, has a growing and diverse student population with 17 different languages being represented in the 2016-2017 school year. A large percentage of this population, almost 75%, has Spanish as their heritage language or are Spanish language speakers. Alameda offers an 'access for all' model for the DP and the CP, with a whole school MYP. In building the CP, therefore, we wanted to be certain to offer targeted language programmes that would both support and enhance the bilingual language development at all levels of competency for our students. As we were focusing our initial career-related pathway on health careers, it became a natural fit to offer a bilingual medical terminology course with an accompanying Certificate of Completion from our community partner, Common Ground International, at the conclusion of the programme. The blended, bilingual nature of the course allows for language development across the continuum of Spanish-English proficiency, while providing the foundation of a career-specific terminology in both, something which none of our students possessed at the time of initiating the programme. Additionally, the LD course offers perspectives and best practices for culturally relevant and effective communication in the health care field, which is a particularly important area of interaction in the highly mobile and migratory populations facing the public health sector in the US today. It is also a global issue that we feel very keenly here in Colorado, and so we deemed it crucial to include it in the CP LD course.

The language portfolio, an IB requirement of the LD course, can be developed by students in any language of their choosing and, while very exciting, it has proven to be quite challenging for students to keep up sustained, individual secondary or tertiary language development outside of a structured language development environment. Because of this, we changed the structuring of support and the corresponding schedule to allow for a language course that would cross both the first and second year of the CP. Students take the bilingual medical terminology course now during the second semester of their first year and the first semester of their final year of the CP. Additionally, the portfolio development needed sustained support and so is scaffolded into both the LD course and the Personal and Professional Skills course, as well as in the Introduction to Health career-related study, which is a course we offer in semester one of the first year of the CP. We have found that it takes a comprehensive, cross-disciplinary, and sustained effort to help students actively engage in the portfolio process and see it as a process and reflection tool, as well as a performance piece.

To really enhance the essential nature of the core in the CP, we extended the language portfolio to add sections dedicated to the Reflective Project (RP) and Service Learning (SL) so that at the end of their programme, students now make a presentation of their learning to an invited panel of community and health sciences-related professionals. This presentation of their learning to a panel has had a profound impact on the whole community as it strengthens bonds between our school programme and the surrounding professional community in a celebratory and meaningful way. Students practise professional presentation skills and learn to effectively respond to questions about their learning and their projects from professionals in the field. The panel members, on the other hand, get to see first-hand the quality of the pre-professional training the students receive and then demonstrate in a summative presentation. I believe this to be one of the most exciting parts of our programme and one we continue to develop along with our students.

The challenges

As we grow and add new career-related studies, such as a creative arts pathway, we are finding that it was a really perfect fit to start with the health sciences because health-related language and communication is such a well-defined field and so it was fairly easy to build it into the CP. This is not so clear for the creative arts pathway, which includes everything from architecture to graphic and digital media arts. As the language offering for this pathway is not as clear cut, we are taking some different approaches and investigating the business language angle. The focus could be business language in the arts, which would highlight interactional language in the professional arts and engineering fields. In the meantime, the language portfolio development is being supported through the development of an art portfolio, and linguistically through the pedagogical approach taken by a CP core teacher who is bilingual English-Turkish, with a third language proficiency in Spanish. She builds strong language identity through culture and art as students process and reflect on art/design-related concepts and terminology.

Another challenge we have faced is finding sufficient time to meet and collaboratively support the language portfolio development through the programme, although I feel we have a successful structure in place currently. But "doing" a portfolio is not the same as "dynamically and reflectively developing" a portfolio, which is our goal. Supporting students understanding of this difference is key and really accelerates the learning when they begin to understand the nature of the portfolio for their learning in this light.

At this juncture in our growth, it think it is valuable to say that what we at Alameda are seeing in our programme is the reflection of natural language development within any given human setting. It is not rigid, as language development is not rigid; it is adaptive and organic, as natural language is adaptive and generative within situated human contexts. As the social linguistic characteristics operating within the different career pathways begin to surface, so too does our understanding of how to structure them within the programme. It is a constantly evolving process, as is language itself. This means it is also more likely to be sustainable, moving into the future, because it is responsive to the changing needs of our complex environment, from within the school to the surrounding career-related fields. The nature of LD in the CP core is well suited to this type of dynamic.

The impact

Language learning in the CP at Alameda is now perceived as purposeful and as an essential element in developing the professional skills that will enable our students to bridge the academic and professional worlds. The language development portfolio is a key piece in this endeavour, and collaboratively building it with the students, at every step of the process, has been exceptionally rewarding. Collaboration in the development of their programme is also a critical skill for students in the professional arena, and so we regularly engage in reflections with them on the efficacy of all elements of our programme. As the students become a greater part of the dynamic process of the development of the CP, so their skills sets develop in a profound and purposeful way, a way that will help them find their place and contribute to the globally connected, socialised world in which they will live. Developing language programmes for specific career-related studies in the CP at Alameda has undoubtedly changed the way our school community sees both language and professional interaction.

References

Genc, C. and Bada, E. (2005): *Culture in language learning and teaching.* The Reading Matrix, 5 (1), pp. 73-84.

Paige, R. M. (2000): *Culture learning in language education: a review of the literature.* Available at: www.google.co.uk/search?hl=en&q=culture+learning+in+language+education%3A+a+revie w+of+the+literature&aq=f&aqi=g1&aql=&oq=&gs_rfai

Rose, C. (2003): *Intercultural learning.* Available at: www.teachingenglish.org.uk/think/articles/ intercultural-learning-1

Part B

Implementing the Career-related Programme in a national context

Chapter 7

The Career-related Programme in the US

Paul Campbell and Natasha Deflorian

Career and technical education in the US

From the early years of the development of the IB Career-related Programme (CP), there was a consensus within the organisation that the US possessed the greatest potential for its widespread adoption. This has proved to be the case, particularly in public (state) schools. However, to understand fully the context, it is useful to consider the complex and often confusing landscape of career and technical education in the country.

As one senior Career and Technical Education (CTE) official said: "You can say anything you want to about career and technical education in the country (the US) and it will be true… somewhere." Unlike many countries in which the IB operates, the standards for CTE in the US are set by individual states instead of a national ministry of education. Along with other factors, such as funding and demographic disparities, this decentralised model has produced a wide spectrum of quality when it comes to the CTE programmes offered at secondary schools. In the worst cases, schools are offering programmes that are deficient in terms of both input (content, standards, assessment, and teacher quality) and output (completion, credentials, chances of accessing employment). Even if they complete these programmes, students often are only prepared for low wage and low skill jobs. Schools ignore the overwhelming amount of research on the 'skills gap'. This frequently used term describes the shortage of high school and university graduates who are being properly prepared for an economy that demands technical expertise and requires employees to communicate and collaborate across cultures.

On the other hand, there are a number of highly demanding and advanced CTE programmes that are spreading quickly throughout the country, particularly in the areas of engineering, finance, and health careers; these programmes are academically rigorous and often require university level mastery of mathematics and science. Most graduates of these programmes proceed directly to four-year university courses, often at highly selective institutions.

To get a glimpse of the conflicting opinions about the value of career education in the US, consider the use of the term 'vocational education'. This term is used in many countries and is understood to mean just what it says: an educational pathway chosen by students who are interested in preparing for a specific career. This is considered a legitimate and educationally sound option. In the

US, however, the term is no longer in general use as it has come to be perceived by the public as describing an education that is somehow less rigorous than a college preparatory programme. Indeed, in comprehensive high schools that offer both college preparation and career education, the two groups of students often are in separate parts of the building and rarely interact. There is also a doctrinal belief in the country that attending university is the most powerful path to prosperity. While it is true that college graduates will earn more over the course of a lifetime than students who do not finish college, this overlooks three important factors. First, while many students start college, there is significant attrition, with current completion rates for university degrees hovering near 60%. According to The Condition of Education 2016 report (National Centre for Educational Statistics, 2016), fewer than 40% of 29 year olds hold a four-year degree.

Secondly, student debt is a fact of life for US students, which is hard to comprehend for people living in countries where university is free or inexpensive. It has been reported that the class of 2016 from four-year universities graduated with an average student loan balance of $37,000, which often takes years to pay off and complicates the career choices of young adults. Finally, while it is clear that a high school diploma is insufficient to participate fully in the information economy, there are several rewarding and well paid jobs that require less than two years of specific technical training.

Several legitimate questions have arisen in education circles in recent years. Is a four-year college education the best path for all students? Should students and their families at least consider the benefits of a rigorous course of CTE study, one that challenges the students while engaging them in something that holds a particular interest? Is it possible to prepare for both college and career? The current desired goal in the US is both college and career readiness. As the CP becomes better known, it would seem to be a natural pathway to achieving this goal. The IB's Diploma Programme (DP) courses that make up part of the CP are considered amongst the best means of preparing for college in the world. The CTE requirement of the CP – the career-related study – ensures that a student will have a meaningful exposure to the knowledge and skills required for demanding careers. Like all IB programmes, there are also the core activities which give the programme its true identity. IB programmes will always demand that students learn to express themselves in a language other their mother tongue, and that they engage in service learning in a serious way. The CP requires both of these, then adds a Personal and Professional Skills course and a Reflective Project to round out a truly rigorous and relevant educational experience that addresses both college and career-readiness.

There are some challenges in implementing the CP in the US. Ironically, the first is that the CP is sometimes a victim of the high value placed on the DP by schools, students, parents and universities. Despite the clearly demonstrated academic challenge provided by the CP, some schools are doing battle with the perception that it is 'IB Lite', suitable for students who can't or won't pursue the full DP. Another challenge is that, while the IB recognises that it does not have expertise in evaluating the quality of various CTE courses, it is important that the quality of these courses in the CP be at a high standard across all CP schools. Lastly, as is always the case with IB programmes in the US state sector, the cost of the CP and the myriad governmental requirements can make implementation of the CP challenging.

However, the same can be, and undoubtedly was, said about the DP, the Middle Years Programme (MYP) and the Primary Years Programme (PYP) in their infancy. Yet all three programmes found widespread acceptance and are transforming schools, students, teachers and communities every day. The same thing is happening in the early years of the CP, and it is by these daily transformations that the true value of the programme will be discovered. As always, it is a story best told by the experience of individual schools and students, including those that follow.

The many shapes and sizes of the CP in US schools

The CP curriculum model provides a flexible framework, allowing schools to develop a programme that truly meets the needs of its students while taking into account the local context. Though the majority of the CP schools in the US are publicly funded, schools in both the private and public sectors have adopted the CP. The CP has been implemented in urban, elite and rural schools, and adopted by individual schools, groups of schools, and across whole districts. Chicago Public Schools, for example, committed to implementing the CP in seven of its high schools which already offered the DP. Since 2012, the district has experienced enormous success with the CP. For the May 2016 IB examination session, the Chicago Public Schools' CP pass rate was 87.5% compared to the world average of 72.5%.

As the CP has now been made available to schools not already offering the DP, the IB is experiencing an increase in the number of technical schools implementing the CP. The state of Pennsylvania has even provided financial assistance to schools interested in implementing the CP as they undertake the process of becoming an authorised IB school. As a result, there are three stand-alone CP candidate schools seeking authorisation in Pennsylvania.

The following case studies demonstrate that the CP is truly not a one-size-fits-all model and that the traditional definition of success is rapidly changing.

School profile: St. Joan Antida

St. Joan Antida (SJA) is an inner city, all-girls private Catholic high school in Milwaukee, Wisconsin. It serves a population in which 98% of students are considered economically disadvantaged and more than 60% are first generation college-bound. In 2013, SJA began the simultaneous DP/CP authorisation process to offer its students more opportunities. "St. Joan Antida High School was a school that was in need of academic direction with a redesign of curriculum that also respected the work we were already doing," says Head of School, Paul Gessner.

The school has been delivering the Project Lead the Way (PLTW) pre-engineering curriculum to its students for years, and partners with the Milwaukee School of Engineering (MSOE) as a part of the programme. Adding the CP allowed the school to combine the existing PLTW offerings with an IB education, thus offering students another choice of programme. "It was important that we remain committed to the pre-engineering programme as a pathway out of poverty for our girls," says Gessner. "We decided that both the DP and the CP needed to be adopted at the same time and we have seen that this decision was the right one."

Now students who are passionate about engineering don't need to choose between the IB and engineering. The CP provides them with the option to get the best of both worlds as they are able to engage in rigorous engineering courses alongside the CP core and DP courses. This well-rounded experience prepares them for opportunities beyond their high school experience. According to Gessner, MSOE plans to recognise the CP as qualifying students for admission into the engineering school.

As an IB World School, every student at SJA is an IB student. The IB philosophy, mission and Learner Profile are embedded in the school culture and have become the underpinnings of what education means inside those walls. Students can thrive in an academically challenging environment, and they are overcoming stigmas they were affiliated with based on their zip code or the colour of their skin. "IB is helping me prove that my children are just as capable of success as the students at the wealthiest schools in Milwaukee," says Gessner.

Overwhelming community support and student engagement have validated the addition of the IB. More than half of SJA senior students (grade 12) are enrolled in the full DP or CP, and the school graduated its first cohort of CP and DP students in May 2017.

School profile: The British International School of Houston

The British International School of Houston (BISH) is a private international school in Houston, Texas. It serves a population of students from varying socio-economic backgrounds and ethnicities. BISH prides itself on providing a personalised, global education for each of its students. The school has offered the DP since 2005, and was authorised to offer the CP in 2012. It decided to add the CP to allow students with a clear career focus to participate in a programme that better suited their academic and professional interests. BISH was one of the first CP schools in the US to be accredited by EdExcel as a BTEC centre. UK-based BTEC qualifications provide students with practical skills development opportunities to prepare them for further studies or to enter directly in to the workforce. By adding the CP, BISH was able to enhance the existing BTEC courses "by embedding the holistic approach that is so fundamental to the IB," says Hayle Byrne, DP/CP coordinator at the school.

BISH students have a variety of BTEC courses to choose from for their career-related study. For example, the school has offered a sports-related course, as well as qualifications in business, engineering, IT, and health and social care. Due to the size of the school it is able to offer options based on student interest, creating individualised learning experiences for all. Since the first CP cohort graduated in 2014, students have gone on to study at many prestigious universities in the US and the UK.

School profile: Rockville High School

Rockville High School is a public school in Rockville, Maryland, and is one of more than twenty IB World Schools in the school district of Montgomery County. It serves a diverse population of nearly fourteen hundred students and houses the county's Deaf and Hard of Hearing Programme. Rockville High School is one of eight DP high schools in the county; it was authorised to offer the DP in 2007 and added the CP in 2012. Since the introduction of IB programmes at Rockville, the school has seen a rapid growth in enrolment. There has been a push across Montgomery County to provide students with opportunities to be academically challenged while also being able to pursue their interests, whether they be in health science, arts, business, culinary arts, digital media or automotive technology. The CP provides CTE students at the school with a chance also to be IB students.

"The CP helped change the meaning of success in the school, breaking down the idea that only the best and brightest will be successful in an IB programme," says Laurie Ainsworth, DP/CP coordinator at Rockville High School. Due to the flexibility of the CP and the focus on a student's career-related studies, the programme intrigues students. Rockville High School has seen a tremendous growth in the number of students participating in the CP. One factor in this growth was the decision to increase the options for the career-related studies available for CP students. At Rockville, students now are able to select from career and technical education pathways that include engineering, culinary arts, child development, justice, law and society, broadcast media and computer science. With such a wealth of options, students with all interests and career aspirations can find a place for themselves. The CP cohort has almost tripled in size since the beginning and now has 70 students.

A student profile

One student, let's call her Anisha, would have settled for the DP had the CP not been an option for her as she entered 11th grade at Watkins Mill High

School in Gaithersburg, Maryland. "She was dead set on the medical profession and passionately wanted to take part in our Medical Careers Academy," says Lisa Ingraham, Watkins Mills High School DP/CP coordinator. "The timing was perfect for her; she was in line to be a member of our first CP graduating cohort, and was able to complete the Medical Academy while participating in a meaningful and exciting new IB programme."

Anisha, like more than half of her classmates at Watkins Mill High School, came from an economically disadvantaged family. Watkins Mill is home to students from many backgrounds, nationalities, religions and mother tongues. Anisha emigrated to the U.S. from Nepal at the age of nine, and was enrolled in a Montgomery County public school where she learned English as a second language. Eight years later, she found herself as an IB student enrolled in the CP which allowed her to engage in academically rigorous courses while following her passion for the medical profession.

As a part of the CP, Anisha studied DP courses in biology, English and physics. As a student in the Medical Careers Academy, she was enrolled in challenging science courses, and completed her medical internship at local hospitals and nursing homes. "Shadowing the doctors and actually doing clinical work was my favourite part of the CP," says Anisha. When she graduated from high school she earned a 3.76 GPA (out of a 4 point scale) and was awarded a prestigious four-year, full-tuition leadership scholarship. In addition to her high school diploma, she received her CNA (Certified Nurse's Assistant) certificate, CPR certification (Cardiopulmonary resuscitation) and the CP.

"Engaging in hands-on experiential learning facilitated relevant connections to her DP and career-related studies courses, giving Anisha the foundation and tools she needed to achieve her goal of becoming a Physician's Assistant," says Linda Mitchell, Academy of Health Professions Coordinator at Watkins Mill. Due to the flexible nature of the CP, Anisha was not bound by scheduling constraints and was afforded the ability to design her schedule in a way that allowed her to focus on her passion, something that the DP would not have offered.

In conclusion, the flexibility of the CP and the emphasis on career-related studies is helping to redefine the meaning of success in today's ever-changing, global marketplace. Through the CP, students are challenged academically and are learning hands-on skills in both their DP and CTE courses. They are also developing essential skills such as critical and ethical thinking, intercultural understanding, collaboration, and effective communication. Through the CP, students are being well prepared both for college and for the world of work.

References

National Centre for Education Statistics (2016): *The Condition of Education 2016*. Washington DC: US Department of Education.

Chapter 8

Bridging the divide through the Career-related Programme in the UK: a leap of faith

David Barrs

The context

It has been a view long held by many in British education that there is a perceptual, if not an actual, divide between a vocational and a more traditional academic education. The former is essentially applied, technical, professional, whilst the latter is based on subject disciplines and is essentially cognitive in nature.

In reality, both should sit comfortably alongside each other in a modern all-ability comprehensive school. Indeed, elements of both should be relevant and fulfilling to most, if not all, students. It is a mistake to consider them as separate and that a divide exists at all. This is, of course, a simplification, but it sets the scene for the decision that the Anglo European School took in 2009 to adopt the International Baccalaureate Career Programme (CP), or International Baccalaureate Career-related Certificate (IBCC), as it was then called.

The Anglo European School is an all ability, state-funded, co-educational comprehensive school with approximately 1,450 students. It is situated in the village of Ingatestone in Essex, England, a village of some 4,000 inhabitants. It embraces the full socio-economic spectrum, but many of its population are commuters working in London. There are also families with an international background that have moved to the village to secure a place at the school.

In 1973, the Local Authority (Essex) had the opportunity to establish a school along European lines when the Ingatestone Secondary Modern School was destined for closure. This had been a policy objective since 1967. 1973 was the year in which the UK joined the Common Market (now the European Union). The first head teacher, Norman Pitt, was appointed and he embarked on the task of defining what a school 'along European lines' actually meant.

Essentially, and looking back on those days, the seeds of the school's 'five pillars' were sown from the outset. These 'pillars' are a fundamental belief in a broad curriculum; the importance of what was originally a European citizenship education, but which grew into global citizenship education; the indispensable value of language learning; and the enriching, character-building contribution of travel abroad and family exchange. The 'fifth pillar' was the mission, values and ethos of the IB, which embraces the other pillars and which provides clear purpose and philosophy to the work of the school. Anglo European started offering the IB Diploma Programme (DP) in 1977 and has done so ever since. The school also offered a British A Level route through its Sixth Form and a hybrid route of A Levels and stand-alone DP courses. All students in the Sixth Form study a language, Citizenship and the CAS (Creativity, Activity and Service) component of the DP. However, it is important to note at this stage that it is the IB mission that drives the school and impacts on all students and staff within the 'Anglo Family' whether they follow the DP or CP route or not. In keeping with the school's belief in breadth, A Level students are expected to follow four rather than three A Levels.

The school has been, from its beginnings, a pioneer of a traditional, liberal education with a modern, deeply embedded international dimension that prepares students well for the global context in which they will increasingly live and work. The school's offer continues to be characterised by breadth, rigour, concurrency of learning, a strong attachment to holistic educational principles and an international ethos that ensures that the outcome of what it does is, for each individual child, more than the sum its parts. A baccalaureate style education, therefore, has been the hallmark of the school since its early days. Indeed, in the absence of an accepted definition of such an approach to education the school has written its own.

A baccalaureate education

"A baccalaureate programme is an educational experience that is broad (involving all major subject disciplines); balanced (in that specialisation is deferred or avoided) and coherent (with clear values, learner outcomes and themes which add relevance to subject study). The programme adds up to more than the sum of its parts and provides for the rounded education of the student.

Learning is concurrent to enable connections to be made and the programme is founded on a very clear set of values. A baccalaureate will also contain a core of learning common to all learners which would typically include individual research, an element of study skills and an opportunity to demonstrate service above self. The core provides an opportunity for learning to be applied as well as to deepen understanding and enrich learning itself. Where appropriate, assessment is rigorous and based on agreed criteria which are not subject to change other than as part of periodic systematic review." (Anglo European School, 2012)

The school's aims reflect this definition and embody the distinctive features, or 'pillars' referred to earlier. The aims and the definition, read together, give an insight into the pioneering history of the school and how it has created its very distinctive provision.

Aims of the Anglo European School

- **Special quality:** To provide the highest quality of education which is enriched by a strong international dimension.

- **Intercultural worth:** To respect individuals and their culture whilst developing a respect for, and an understanding of, the student's own culture and the cultures of others.

- *L'Avenir*: To give students the academic and social skills which enable them to move freely and productively beyond the boundaries of their own community.

(Anglo European School – www.aesessex.co.uk)

The school had attempted to broaden its Sixth Form provision previously in order to make it relevant to a wider range of our students, as well as students from other schools. In 2001 the school appointed a senior member of staff to introduce vocational courses. BTEC Sport and GNVQ languages were a key feature of the offer. Staff were trained, accreditation received, and structures put in place. Sadly, after two attempts to recruit sufficient students, the project was abandoned, although other vocational courses continued to enrich the language offer which had to meet the needs of students across the ability range.

Our students and, importantly, our parents, saw vocational courses as a poor partner to the traditional academic route represented by the DP and A Levels. Arguably, the DP was embraced with some enthusiasm in 1977 not simply because it was a progressive, outward-looking programme that was predicated on international mindedness, but because it was increasingly seen as an excellent preparation for university. University has always been the predominant destination for Anglo European School students. 90%+ progress to university; 70%+ get to their first choice and 40%+ go to Russell Group institutions (some of the top universities in the UK). Rightly or wrongly, the view seemed to be that the vocational route wasn't a route to university.

Implementing the CP

The global pilot for the CP, led by the visionary Chris Mannix, then head of the CP at the IB, was well underway when the news of its existence reached Ingatestone. This news was received with some excitement by the senior leaders and staff. Could it be the answer to the school's desire to broaden the intake of its Sixth Form? Could the CP bridge the divide between the academic and the vocational? Could it enable a wider range of young people to benefit from a Sixth Form experience at the Anglo European School? Could it complement both the A Level programme and the DP? Could it become the first state school in the UK to offer it, as we had offered the DP over 30 years previously? The school was also acutely aware that the government had decided to raise the age for students leaving education to 18 from 2015. The importance of broadening the Sixth Form, therefore, became a matter of policy imperative and economics as well as a genuine desire to make the post-16 educational offer relevant to a wider range of students.

The excitement was borne of the view that a vocational programme had a much greater chance of success if it was backed by an organisation with a reputation for academic excellence, which was well regarded by universities and which was also highly regarded for its rigour and the absence of examination grade inflation which had hampered the reputation of A Levels. Indeed, there were those who regarded UK vocational courses as a way of inflating examination performance, a view which is still held by some.

From the outset, Anglo European School was encouraged by the IB to become involved in the CP pilot. We were a state school, we were in the UK and we were well-regarded within the IB community. Yet the pilot was already well established with ten schools worldwide and it took the courage of Chris Mannix to embrace our enthusiasm. He did so with his customary decency, humour and passion. Three colleagues were duly dispatched to the conference of pilot schools in Dubai (March 2010), itself a cause of some excitement for a state school whose professional development budget was, and still is, inadequate.

Given the above, the context of the school and its pioneering philosophy, Anglo European was well placed to embrace the CP. However, the CP was a radical departure from our traditional provision and its introduction would need careful management. It was also a brave decision in that there were at that point no national agreements on funding or UCAS tariff equivalence in terms of UK school league tables. Recognition by the Office of Qualifications and Examinations Regulation (Ofqual) came in September 2011, one year after the school started teaching its first CP cohort. This, of course, was a significant step for all schools worldwide given the status of Ofqual, but it was certainly important for the Anglo European School to offer a programme which was regulated by them. In December 2011, the school was part of a delegation to the Young People's Learning and Skills Agency in Coventry, UK, where the case for appropriate funding was successfully made.

These national decisions vindicated our own decision to introduce the CP, but also underlined how brave the school's decision was. Had those national decisions gone the other way, the school would have been left in a very difficult position even though we knew we had an exciting and relevant programme for our students.

The challenges

In introducing the CP the school faced some key challenges: the perception of vocational courses held by our parents, students and staff; the recognition of the programme by the higher education and funding authorities; the definition of what were considered acceptable career-related studies by the IB; and the prior learning achievements the school would require before a student was allowed on the CP.

1. Perception

Given the school's previous experience of vocational courses, this was a key consideration. The ability to promote the CP as part of the IB suite of programmes was very important. Nevertheless, there were still parents who regarded it as an inappropriate programme with regard to progression to university. Some had conducted their own research and reached the conclusion that the CP was not for their child. There continues to be an issue whereby staff teaching DP Standard Level courses as part of the full DP also have to meet the needs of students who are following the CP; teaching students from two different programmes in one class continues to prove challenging for some.

2. Recognition

At the time of its inception, recognition of the new CP by higher education institutions was a real issue and the school's decision, therefore, was very much a leap of faith. This was clearly a factor in the conclusion being reached by some parents. The key stakeholders (Ofqual, universities, UCAS and the funding authorities) were yet to make a clear declaration in favour of the CP. This had to wait until Autumn 2012. In the meantime the school had to rely on the fact that the two applied A Levels it had put forward as the career-related study component of the CP, and the stand alone DP Standard Level courses, which had been part of the school's hybrid offer for many years, were well-regarded by universities and appropriately funded. At the time of writing, the CP is recognised by Ofqual as a Level 3 course, by UCAS (including UCAS Apply), by over 100 UK universities and it is registered in the UK Qualifications Guide and the International Qualifications Guide used by UK universities. Our own CP students have gained places at 20 universities partly because of the grades they have achieved and partly because the CP is an IB programme.

3. Definition

The school was pleased that the IB recognised Applied A Levels as an appropriate vocational qualification for the career-related study component of the CP. The accepted vocational courses in the UK, such as BTEC, had been tried at the school previously without success. A further debate with the IB as to why A Levels such as Physical Education and Design Technology could not be regarded as vocational was had, but without a positive conclusion. At the time of writing, the future of Applied A Levels in the UK is in question and the school is looking at alternatives including Cambridge Technicals and the Certificate in Financial Studies offered by the UK Institute of Financial Studies. With London's financial sector so close, this qualification is of significant interest to the school.

4. Requirements to study the CP (matriculation)

A key decision for the school was to decide the level at which the school should pitch the programme in terms of prior qualifications and entry requirements.

To obtain a place on the CP it was decided that students would be required to obtain C grades in four subjects at GCSE, including English, but B grades in the subjects they wished to study at A Level, and C grades in the chosen DP Standard Level subjects. This would open up the programme to a wider range of students, although there is always scope for the use of discretion in certain circumstances. For instance, discretion would be needed for the large number of students who apply to the Anglo European School Sixth Form from outside the UK, often without GCSE qualifications.

Our first decision was to decide on our vocational offer which would become the career-related study component of the CP. The IB had taken the brave step of recognising local vocational qualifications as part of one of the CP, and had reached an agreement with BTEC, now run by Pearson, which endorsed the courses as being appropriate to sit within the CP. Unfortunately, given the school's earlier experience of BTEC courses, it meant we had to think very carefully about how this was approached. A decision was made, therefore, following discussions with the IB, to position Applied A Levels in our vocational core. A broad choice was available: business studies, ICT, applied science, health and social care, travel and tourism and textiles. In order to ensure breadth and a viable basis for university application at a time when Ofqual had not guaranteed recognition of the CP, the school also insisted on a second Applied A Level for entry to the CP. The Sixth Form team took the approach that the target group for CP would be any student who had chosen any of the above Applied A Level courses. They would then be interviewed with a view to wrapping the CP qualification around their Applied A Level choice.

A decision was also taken at that time to require all students on the programme to organise and participate in an internship in a work environment. The school had a strong tradition of promoting work experience for pre-Sixth Form students and wanted to build on this experience with this new programme. It also coincided with a view from government that work experience should be encouraged at Sixth Form level following the publication of the Wolf Report (Department for Education, 2011) in the UK on vocational education.

Reflecting on the implementation of the process

Mitigating the risks

In summary, the introduction of the CP was straightforward, though not without the risks alluded to above. It was a qualification that could be wrapped around offers that already existed at the Anglo European School. The all-important CP core (Personal and Professional Skills; Service Learning; Language Development; the Reflective Project), the key to bridging the vocational/academic divide, was innovative but not radical as far as the school was concerned. The CAS component of the DP was a well-established part of the offer for all Sixth Formers, albeit defined slightly differently for the

CP, with a greater emphasis on service; language study was already a school requirement for every student; and the Personal and Professional Skills course mirrored the provision we made for Theory of Knowledge for the DP students. The Reflective Project, similarly, mirrored in practical terms the DP Extended Essay.

The school also had experience of the Extended Project Qualification (EPQ) which was becoming increasingly common in UK Sixth Forms. However, as an ethics-based project, the Reflective Project complemented and enriched the school's values-driven ethos which encourages all students to engage with controversial issues. Some of the topics chosen for the Reflective Projects give a sense of the challenge involved: is it ethical to offer micro-credit to those on very low incomes in less economically developed countries? Is the beauty myth unethical? Is FIFA (international governing body of football) unethical? Should the promotion of payday lending schemes be restricted? Should zero hours contracts be banned? Should cyber-bullying be a crime? Should Stansted Airport be expanded? Should multinational, inclusive resorts be required to give back to the local community?

The risk of implementing the CP was also calculated in that the school undertook research with universities to gauge their response to the programme. We found there was unease and no consensus amongst them about how the CP would be treated; there was, after all, no UK national qualifications or funding recognition for the CP at that stage. However, once our approach to the CP, based on Applied A Levels, was shared with the universities, their response was much more positive. The recruiting-focused as opposed to the selecting-focused universities were particularly receptive. Our conclusion was that a CP student would be in a stronger position than a weak DP or A Level student, partly because of the nature of the A Levels they would have studied, but also because of the uniqueness of the CP core which would enable a student who was relatively weak academically to stand out. The link with the IB was also considered to be an enhancement to the curriculum vitae of a CP student. The school was experienced in dealing with universities who didn't understand the DP and would apply that experience to the benefit of its university-bound CP students.

Reaping the benefits

An unintended benefit of the process of introducing the CP was that it enabled us to engage with the IB organisation and its staff in a more creative and professional manner than previously. Having engaged actively with the IB in the 1970s with the introduction of the DP, more recent engagement had at best been information-seeking or, at worst, reactive when a concern or a complaint had to be aired. In introducing the CP, the Anglo European School worked closely with many committed, experienced and enthusiastic IB staff who seemed set on adopting a 'can-do 'approach to the challenges that the pilot CP schools presented them with.

The school contributed to a number of conferences at a national and international level, the UK IB Schools and Colleges Association (IBSCA) actively sought its advice and colleagues took part in surveys, telephone conferences and Skype calls. One outcome was a Memorandum of Understanding agreed with the IB to offer briefing sessions to interested schools. For many years we had responded to such requests from schools in relation to the DP and the agreement built on this expertise, attracting interest from as far afield as Angola.

The school also provided the context and venue for a CP promotional film which featured one of our students. This student was in our first cohort of CP students; he was spotted and invited to perform at an IB regional conference in 2013. For his CP he studied music at A Level, DP *ab initio* Spanish and applied business A Level, before going on to study commercial music at university.

One particular contribution the Anglo European School was able to make to the development of the CP involved giving our advice on a number of contentious issues which emerged during the process. An early question from the IB was whether or not we thought the CP would cannibalise the DP. This question suggested a concern within the IB itself about the future of the DP. For the school, however, it suggested a fundamental lack of understanding of the contribution the CP could make as a post-16, pre-university programme to the education of succeeding generations of young people. It was important to see the CP as a complement to the DP rather than a competitor, appealing to young people with different aptitudes and interests, rather than a programme designed for the less academic. Indeed, such a view assumes the DP is just for the traditionally academic and the CP for the traditionally less academic. That is not a view which should have credence in a comprehensive school.

This concern echoed the tension in the UK about vocational educational. The 1944 Education Act sponsored by the then Conservative Secretary of State for Education, R A Butler, enshrined the academic/vocational division, and ultimately the tension, by creating grammar schools, accessed by a test at age 11, secondary modern schools and secondary technical schools, the latter being essentially vocational schools. Whilst it also allowed for comprehensive schools that would embrace all three types of school, very few were formed until the Labour Government set out legislation to render all schools comprehensive schools in 1965, although they did not seek to abolish all grammar schools.

Another question that came from many UK schools about the CP was why languages should be part of the compulsory CP core. UK schools have always faced challenges in offering and successfully teaching languages. It is not a matter for this chapter, but it relates to an attitude towards learning languages other than English, the global predominance of English as a working language and the difficulties in recruiting languages teachers. As a school that believes it is a myth that the British are not good at languages, and which requires all of its students to study two languages other than English up to age 16, and at least one in the Sixth Form, we argued strongly that languages had to be part of the CP. It was untenable to offer an international qualification without some requirement to study languages. If that meant a school could not offer the CP then they would still have the option of offering A Levels, with or without a language.

Until recently, IB promotional materials failed to make reference to the four IB programmes, continuing to reference only the DP, the MYP and the Primary Years Programme (PYP). This created obstacles to the school positively promoting the CP, but the issue has now been resolved and the CP sits comfortably alongside the other three IB programmes. The CP has taken rightful place in the IB continuum of international education, enabling a much wider range of young people to benefit from the IB experience which, in turn, enables them to make a positive impact on the world, rendering it, hopefully, a better place.

Looking back, adopting the CP was, indeed, a leap of faith both for the Anglo European School and the IB, but one which has been vindicated by the numbers of young people benefiting from the programme, moving on to university or work, and making a difference. Students like Ben who went on to the University of Manchester, Ellie who studied Applied Science as her career-related study and went on to do forensic science, and Josh who went on to study at Portsmouth University It has enabled the school to enlarge its Sixth Form and enabled more students, both from within the school and increasingly from elsewhere, to enjoy the full impact of an international education at the Anglo European School.

References

Anglo European School (nd): *The Aims of Anglo European School.* Available at: www.aesessex. co.uk

Wolf, A. (2011): *Review of Vocational Education.* London, UK: Department for Education.

Chapter 9

A collaborative approach to implementing the Career-related Programme: the Kent pilot schools in the UK

Tony Smith

The group pilot of the IB Career-related Programme (CP), which took place in Kent, a county in south-east England, was based on a belief that innovation benefits from collaboration within networks of schools. This provides mutual support, disseminates good practice rapidly and promotes sustainability. The pilot, which ran from 2010 to 2015, was intended to demonstrate that, by collaboration, the CP could be developed successfully in schools which, in their present situations, could not give serious consideration to the introduction of the IB Diploma Programme (DP). This CP pilot widened access to a post-16 education, offering an IB education to students who did not have the opportunity to choose the DP and who attended schools that operate in difficult circumstances. The design of a model to meet local conditions was a key feature of the pilot, and reflected an awareness that it is such an approach that enables a global brand to flourish.

The Model

The concept of the pilot was of a hub with spokes. The hub was a state-funded IB World School: Dane Court Grammar School, which offered the DP and, at the time when the pilot was planned, had decided to introduce the CP. The spokes consisted of Kent high schools which had no experience of the DP. The network was led, supported and co-ordinated by staff at Dane Court Grammar School, through which the 'spoke' schools entered candidates for examinations in IB subjects until they could themselves be authorised as IB World Schools.

Experience of schools' development of both the DP and the IB Middle Years Programme (MYP) influenced the planning of the pilot. In the case of the DP, external support from the IB comes mainly during the phase of candidacy. Once authorisation to offer the DP has been achieved, a school is likely to operate independently. However thorough the preparation, and even where there is a sub-regional organisation, such as the IB Schools and Colleges Association of the UK (IBSCA) offering support, each new DP school faces challenges that may be greater than anticipated, for example in the judgement of standards required and in relation to the demands made on students in terms of their workload. A further issue is that a change of leadership can threaten the future of the programme within the school. There has been a pattern in England of schools gaining authorisation to offer the DP and then discontinuing it before it has had an opportunity to become established. The schools, to justify their decisions, tend to become hostile and vocal critics of the DP and of the IB in general, and this can create difficulties for other DP schools in marketing the programme. Such disadvantages are unlikely to result from the MYP approach to authorisation, which takes place after the programme is established and has been offered, with external support, for several years. The 'hub and spoke' model provided the necessary support until participating schools, by the time of authorisation, had sustainable CP programmes and extended experience of operating as a network. The model's potential weakness was the extent of reliance on the altruism of Dane Court Grammar School. The pilot's success is, therefore, a tribute to the dedication of that school's visionary Executive Head Teacher, Paul Luxmoore. Highly committed to the IB and its philosophy (and a key member of the Steering Committee of IBSCA), he believes in the CP's capacity not only to transform education for many students, but also to aid economic regeneration for the local area.

The Context

The Isle of Thanet is part of Kent, and no longer technically an island. Dane Court Grammar School is one of this coastal district's seven state secondary schools, and one of the two which are selective, known as grammar schools. The other five are referred to as high schools. Thanet is one of the most deprived areas of south-east England, with relatively high unemployment, and considered to be characterised by low aspirations and insularity. The many challenges for its schools include their admitting a very high proportion of students with English as an additional language, and an exceptional number of looked-after children, living away from their parents in foster care arranged by local authorities, particularly the London boroughs. Kent is one of the two largest local authorities in England, with approximately one hundred state secondary schools. It is a diverse county, combining areas of affluence, particularly in the west, with areas of deprivation. The latter are found on its extensive coastline and along the south bank of the River Thames, but also exist in some rural parts of the county and in specific urban housing estates. Kent retains selection of pupils at the age of eleven, with twenty-five percent admitted to grammar schools, and the remainder to high schools. The process can benefit those who are selected to attend grammar schools, but tends to damage the self-esteem of others and to restrict their aspirations.

The ability range of students in Kent high schools, and their relatively low post-16 numbers, would prevent it being cost-effective for them to attempt to offer the DP. More able students in high schools are likely to be drawn to grammar schools for post-16 study (even if their previous experience does not represent suitable preparation for this). The CP, however, because of its flexibility, suits the high schools extremely well if introduced and developed appropriately.

The main post-16 academic qualification in England, Wales and Northern Ireland is the Advanced Level of the General Certificate of Education (A Level), with students choosing separate subjects from a large menu of courses. While many Kent high schools have offered A Level courses, most of their post-16 students have taken vocational courses with or without A Levels in addition. Success rates in the vocational subjects have tended to be good, but A Level results have often been disappointing, particularly where those courses are combined with vocational subjects. This may reflect the contrasting learning styles of the schools' vocational and academic courses. The reform of A Levels, with a national policy of making them more difficult, is likely to reduce their suitability for students in Kent high schools still further. Where A Level courses have been introduced, the need to build viable numbers has led high schools to choose academic subjects likely to appeal to students, rather than those which would be of the greatest value to them and maximise their chances of success. While some high schools have developed coherent programmes for their students, many have not, providing an assortment of diverse elements. There are examples of successful practice, but the effectiveness of high schools' preparation of students for higher education is often limited.

The CP has a unique appeal for Kent high schools. It offers a coherent approach to post-16 education and combines academic and career-related (vocational) studies with a core of personal and social development. The Personal and Professional Skills course enables students to understand themselves as learners, and to reconcile the contrasting demands of academic and vocational study. The programme's flexibility allows individual needs to be met successfully, for example in the range of career-related alternatives available, and in the opportunity for students to choose from two to four DP courses, from any DP subject group or groups, at Standard or Higher Level. The CP has demonstrated its capacity to improve student outcomes, raise their aspirations and increase employability. The programme also promotes enterprise and international awareness.

The pilot's success has been gratifying to those involved in it. While its approach has been strategic and systematic, it may be said to have originated from a chance meeting in 2010. A senior educator from Kent, at that time seconded from Dartford Grammar School to the Specialist Schools and Academies Trust, met an IB officer who mentioned that the IB was working on the development of a Career-related Certificate, and planning to pilot it internationally in a few IB World Schools. The potential of the IBCP was quickly understood and Kent County Council was contacted. Subsequently, a meeting between the IB and representatives from Kent County Council was arranged to discuss and agree the concept of a group CP pilot in Kent, involving non-IB World Schools.

By 2010, there was already a high level of commitment to IB programmes in some Kent schools. The DP had become established in grammar schools and independent schools, but the only attempt to introduce it into a non-selective school had failed. In the foreseeable future, it was extremely unlikely that the DP could be offered in a non-selective school in Kent. The CP, however, seemed to represent a new and exciting opportunity to those seeking an expansion of an IB education in the county.

Implementation

Following the meeting with the IB, a group of four coastal high schools was brought together in June, 2010, and possible involvement in an CP pilot was discussed. Three of the schools were on Thanet, and the fourth a short distance to the south of it. The participants were invited to work in partnership, with Dane Court Grammar School as a hub, entering candidates through the hub until ready themselves for IB authorisation. Eventually, three of the high schools agreed to be involved. Funding was sought from Kent County Council to support the pilot, and obtained on the condition that high schools in other parts of the county could also take part. Four more high schools joined the potential pilot group, providing a total of seven spokes to the hub. While it would have been advantageous for all of the high schools to have been reasonably close to the hub, the additional schools were between 35 and 65 miles away from Thanet. It was, however, at that stage envisaged that the high schools would, when authorised by the IB, become hubs themselves, with further spokes attached to them. Inclusion of the more distant participants was intended to be part of a strategic approach to the development of a network of CP schools across the county.

Preparations continued through the summer and autumn of 2010, in consultation with the IB and the Kent County Council. Five of the schools prepared to offer the CP from September 2011, with support from Dane Court Grammar School, and began to recruit students, while the other two planned to introduce the programme in September, 2012. Details of the pilot were finalised in December 2010, and it was launched officially in the following February with an evening event, addressed by George Walker, the former Director General of the IB, and authorised training of the seven CP co-ordinators by the IB. The event and the training both took place at The Turner Contemporary, a world-class gallery, which was to open in Margate in April 2011. The choice seemed ideal, as the gallery and the CP were both seen as transformational and international, and as aspects of the economic regeneration of Thanet.

For the rest of the academic year the pilot schools worked together, with external support from the local authority. The co-ordinators met monthly, at Dane Court Grammar School, whose DP Co-ordinator convened and chaired the meetings. The agendas included course-planning, especially of the core, with the Approaches to Learning course (the forerunner to Personal and Professional Skills), Service Learning and Language Development all important priorities. A pattern was set for the joint practice development which was a major feature of the pilot, with co-ordinators sharing their experience and reflections frankly and constructively. They constituted a forum in which no one was afraid to admit concerns and to seek help and advice. All recognised themselves to be learners, having to take risks, but knowing that they need not do this in isolation.

Specific DP courses were recommended to the schools, to reflect their current strengths and the interests of their students. The pilot schools initially chose from that list: business and management, film, information technology in a global society, social and cultural anthropology, and mathematical studies. This focusing on a narrow range can promote the development of subject groupings for mutual support, and assists the provision for moderation of assessments to ensure that teachers' expectations are sound. Authorised subject workshops, with leaders chosen by the IB, were hosted by Dane Court Grammar School in June, 2011. The quality of the workshops was high, and the confidence of the teachers about to introduce the courses was enhanced. Wherever possible, the subject teachers were linked with their counterparts in authorised DP schools for ongoing support.

The first CP students in Kent, from five of the pilot schools, began the programme in September 2011. Within a short time, the schools were reporting the positive impact on students' self-confidence and aspirations, as well as their capacity to cope well with the academic demands of the programme. The other two pilot schools introduced the programme in 2012, as did Dane Court Grammar School. From the point when the first cohort completed the CP in 2013, with 100% of candidates awarded the certificate, success rates have remained high, though the number of entries and the range of subjects offered have increased year by year.

The schools chose one of two models for delivery of the programme. The more common initial approach was to position the DP courses and the CP core (Personal and Professional skills, Service Learning, Language Development and the Reflective Project) in the timetable so that they could be accessed from as many career-related studies as possible. The alternative was to create pathways involving the choice of DP courses to complement a specific career-related study. It had the advantage of ensuring that the students remained together for most of the week, forming a close and supportive group, and developing in accordance with the IB Learner Profile. The model also facilitated the formation of a close relationship between the core and the other elements of the programme. As the pilot has progressed, and numbers of CP students have grown, schools have become increasingly aware of the advantages of career-related pathways. These relate not only to recruitment and retention of students, but also to the ways in which they encourage enrichment and the formation of business links. They are cost-effective, and assist the linking of Language Development and Service Learning with the career-related study chosen. One example is the development of a pathway suitable for a career in finance, with a career-related study in business combined with DP courses in Mathematical Studies, and Information Technology in a Global Society. Another example, which might be appropriate preparation for nursing, is a career-related study in Health and Social Care combined with DP courses in Biology, Psychology or Social and Cultural Anthropology. A third example, leading to a possible career in the creative industries, is a career-related study in the Performing Arts combined with DP courses in Studies in Language and Literature, and Film.

The network continued to develop. The co-ordinators met regularly to share effective practice and to discuss issues relating to the programme's delivery. This collaboration enabled individual schools to manage the process of inducting new co-ordinators, as teachers moved on to new posts. It also assisted the management of changes within the pilot group, which were always likely owing to the nature of the schools involved and their challenging circumstances. One school dropped out in the first year, following a change of head teacher, and another in the second year as a result of internal difficulties. Five of the initial seven schools remained, and were joined by three more, at a rate of one per year, introducing the CP in 2013, 2014 and 2015 respectively. The pilot schools were supported, not only by Dane Court Grammar School but also by other Kent DP schools, providing subject expertise and moderation of standards and assessments. Through the hub school, the pilot members had contact with IBSCA, as well as with the IB. Two consultants from IBSCA were engaged to conduct annual reviews of the pilot schools' provision, in order to assure the quality of provision and guide their continuous improvement towards to a point when they could be authorised as IB World Schools, offering the programme in their own right.

Communication between the IB and the pilot schools was temporarily disrupted in 2014, and the lack of any explicit written agreement between the pilot schools and the IB proved a problem. The exciting discussions that had taken place with regard to a strategic expansion of the pilot had not been recorded formally; consequently, the beginning of a process to authorise the earliest pilot schools was delayed, and a temporary loss of momentum that resulted from this was reflected in uneven growth in the rate of participation within individual schools.

While the IB was supportive of the pilot, and recognised its success, it presented a difficulty for the organisation. The IB, in each of its programmes, is committed to a single system of authorisation for global use. The pilot followed an approach based on that for the MYP, while the IB decided that the CP should follow the approach of the DP, in which introduction of the programme could come only after authorisation at the end of an extended period of preparation during candidacy. The inclusion of DP course in the CP justified this decision. While the pilot schools were disappointed that they would not, after authorisation, be able themselves to act as hubs, extending the network to other parts of Kent, the organisers could see the logic of the IB's view. They were also aware of the extent to which the pilot depended on the support of Dane Court Grammar School, which was unlikely to be replicated elsewhere. In 2015, the IB took a decision to end the pilot, with the acceptance of a final school. A process of authorisation of the pilot schools began, and by the end of June, 2016, the first six had become IB World Schools offering the CP. It seems significant that the beginning of the authorisation process for the pilot schools coincided with an increased focus on the marketing of the CP and a rapid growth in recruitment of students.

The Next Stage

By 2015, the pilot had achieved its aims by proving that the CP could be developed successfully in schools not offering the DP, and extending post-16 IB access to students who would not have been able to take the DP. In October, 2015, Kent's Corporate Director for Education and Young People's Services went to The Hague for a meeting with the IB's Director General. They agreed a Kent project to build on the pilot's success. It was to involve at least ten non-selective schools, that would prepare collaboratively as candidate schools, with support from the IB, and follow an accelerated path to authorisation, so that they would be able to offer the CP from September, 2017. When schools were recruited for the project, the target of ten was exceeded. The schools included both of those that had dropped out of the pilot, and one that had, in 2010, rejected an invitation to participate in it. All three had become aware of the advantages of seizing opportunities previously missed.

As the organisers have drawn on experience of the pilot, the project is based on a shared understanding of the need for effective communication, involving a single point of contact between the project schools and the IB. A co-ordinator, appointed by the local authority, is working with a project leader appointed by the IB, who has a team of trained consultants, each supporting a group of schools. The participating schools form a network and their head teachers are represented by a steering committee. The project features a systematic programme of leadership development and cluster workshops, which are intended to promote establishment of sustainable subject groups. Marketing, both internal and external, is understood by all to be a key feature of planning. A clear timetable will lead to authorisation by an agreed date, in time for the introduction of the CP in 2017.

Lessons Learnt

The CP fulfilled the pilot schools' shared wish to develop a programme that meets their students' need for a coherent preparation for life and careers in an international context. In addition to the intrinsic merits of the programme, which include the flexibility to adapt to personal requirements and a capacity to promote creativity, one can see a variety of other reasons for the pilot's success. The first is the determination, perseverance and resilience of the senior leaders, co-ordinators and teachers involved, principled risk-takers inspired by the philosophy of the IB. A second is the commitment of Dane Court Grammar School, where governors were ready to use its resources in order to benefit other schools, in accordance with Paul Luxmoore's vision. A third is the adoption of a collaborative approach, with schools and their teachers working together in a network for mutual benefit, sharing their expertise, experiences and insights. A fourth is the support provided by the Kent County Council (which quickly grasped the strategic potential of the CP), IBSCA and IB officers.

The pilot provided a number of lessons, which are influencing approaches in the new Kent project. A positive lesson was the power of creating networks by developing a team of co-ordinators across schools and offering joint DP subject training. This can assist schools in managing staff changes. A second lesson is the effectiveness of regular external monitoring and evaluation after the programme has been introduced. However thorough preparation may appear to be, advice and support are needed in the early stages of a programme's operation within a school. Some lessons, however, arose from weaknesses in the planning. Schools should have been given greater support with marketing and recruitment, for example, and governors should have been involved at an earlier stage. Too much reliance was placed on the co-ordinators, instead of bringing together head teachers on a regular basis. Had a network of head teachers been developed, changes in leadership and issues in individual schools would have been less problematic.

Some Words of Advice

The new Kent project reflects the advice that those involved in the original CP pilot would offer other schools. This advice is concerned not only with curriculum and leadership within an individual school, but also with the ways in which schools can work together.

Curriculum

In the individual school, the advice would be to adapt the CP to suit local circumstances and choose career-related studies that match employment opportunities.

- In selecting suitable DP courses, there are advantages in considering the specific demands of each, as well as the curricular area into which they fall.

- If possible, the DP courses should complement the career-related study and offer a career -related pathway, while still keeping a student's options open so that an alternative route might be chosen later. This can lead to greater coherence, with a close relationship between the academic studies, career-related studies and the CP core. By keeping the students together for most of the week, it also promotes collaborative learning and the retention of students.

- The CP core can enable schools to bridge the gap in learning styles between academic and vocational studies.

- The development of DP courses in schools which would not otherwise have been able to introduce them encourages innovation in their delivery. The process prompts teachers to reconsider issues of teaching and learning. They find this stimulating, and schools report that the process affects positively the work of those teachers with other year groups. The IB Learner Profile enables the schools to develop a more consistent approach to the education that they offer throughout the full age range.

Leadership

In terms of leadership, it is important to create a strong and sustainable structure:

- It is valuable to involve governors from the start, rather than simply providing them with information and securing their approval. The commitment and active engagement of a school's governors, particularly of their chair, can ensure that expenditure on the CP is seen as investment in a programme that is not simply an alternative set of examination courses. It can also help the governing body to manage a smooth change of head teacher which will not affect CP provision. Many governors are likely to have links with business, and can assist a school in forming links that will enrich CP provision. When an event was held to introduce the new CP Kent project to schools that might participate, head teachers were invited to attend with their chairs of governors, and this has proved to be beneficial.

- Within a school, it is advantageous to have a leadership team for the CP, rather than to rely only on the CP co-ordinator. Responsibility can be distributed, for example by appointment of members of staff to lead Service Learning and the Reflective Project. This increases teachers' involvement, and can assist the school with succession planning, so that it can cope with a change of CP co-ordinator.

- It is sometimes suggested that the CP co-ordinator should be a member of the school's Senior Leadership Team. This will not always be the case as, at least in the early stages of CP development, the students taking the programme may be a relatively small proportion of the post-16 cohort. It is, however, essential that the CP has a strong advocate within the Senior Leadership Team, and the identification of a Senior Leader as the 'CP Champion' is strongly recommended. If the school offers more than one post-16 programme, one of which is the CP, the head teacher cannot be seen to favour one above the other(s). The 'Champion' needs to have no such inhibition in showing a preference, and can market the CP vigorously.

Collaboration

With regard to collaboration, the advice is particularly strong. Successful introduction of any IB programme depends on risk-takers at every level in a school.

- A network of CP schools assists the management of risks. In the case of head teachers, this provides mutual support, and reduces the feelings of isolation. A network of co-ordinators can accelerate their individual development, disseminate good practice and promote joint problem-solving.

- A network of subject teachers can share innovations, moderate standards and reduce their workload through collaborative planning.

- The ideal structure would seem to be small groupings of schools close enough to each other geographically to make collaboration relatively easy, within a wider network in which the scale is likely to offer greater access to particular expertise.

- The linking of established DP schools to the network can give it even greater effectiveness, and may stimulate reviews within the DP schools of their own approaches.

Final Thoughts

In the pilot, the CP offered multiple benefits to the schools involved: changing their cultures, encouraging them to have a global perspective; promoting consideration of the purposes and effective pedagogy of post-16 education; building social capital; providing a prestigious status that enhances their corporate self-esteem and supports their marketing. Teachers have reviewed their practice, leading to a deeper understanding of teaching and learning, and have gained an awareness that their students can achieve highly by global standards. It is easy to show the pilot's success in terms of examination results and award of certificates. What is most memorable, however, is the way in which the pilot changed students' lives, helping them to become reflective learners and raising their aspirations. A high proportion of the students gained university places when some had not previously considered higher education possible, although many preferred to accept high level apprenticeships, having given themselves an edge over other applicants. The programme also developed their self-confidence, enterprise skills and international-awareness. The CP, by its very nature, differs from the IB's other programmes as, by offering schools flexibility, it thrives when allowed to evolve in a local context. The pilot demonstrated this, and, in doing so, showed the CP's capacity to transform students, teachers and schools.

Chapter 10

Good education changes lives: the Career-related Programme in a UK state school

Kate Greig

It is fitting to begin this chapter on the IB Career-related Programme (CP) and King Ethelbert School in the UK with the knock on my door at 3.20pm on a Friday afternoon by one of our Year 13 students, let's call her Rachel (18 years old). She had received her CP results two days before and had been awarded three distinction stars in her career-related study, an applied science qualification (BTEC Science level 3), a grade 6 in IB Diploma Programme (DP) Mathematics Standard Level, a grade 4 in her DP Psychology Standard Level, and a B in her CP Reflective Project, giving her a much deserved CP diploma and the grades needed for the next stage of her academic studies. Rachel knocked on my door to tell me that she had secured an offer at the University of Loughborough, UK, to study Automotive and Aeronautical Engineering. She was only one of many to do very well and to achieve the grades needed for her chosen post-18 pathway, but Rachel encapsulated for me exactly what the CP offers our students. She was not the first student from King Ethelbert to go to university, nor will she be the last, but before I explain exactly why the story of Rachel is quite remarkable I need to explain about our school.

The context: King Ethelbert Secondary School

King Ethelbert Secondary School is on the Isle of Thanet, in the county of Kent, England. Anyone who knows Thanet will know that it is at the very eastern tip of England. Kent, often referred to as the 'Garden of England', is indeed a place of beauty with leafy towns in the west and a stretch of coastline that includes the famous white cliffs of Dover and the historic dockyards of Chatham. It has wealth, privilege and an interesting history, but it also has poverty, deprivation and some of the extremes of the social class structure. Thanet has a history of low educational achievement which, inevitably, affects the aspirations of its young people. Teenage pregnancy figures are high and the proportion of the population going to university is low (11% in the catchment area of our school). The percentage of students across Thanet applying for free school meals, a key indicator of social and economic deprivation in the UK, is well over 50%, and the percentage of families who are fourth generation unemployed is not insignificant. Kent, and therefore Thanet, has a selective system of education which means that all students take an examination at the age of 11. 30% of the most able then attend local, selective grammar schools;

the rest go to non-selective schools and King Ethelbert is one of these. King Ethelbert is not a traditional secondary school such as can be found across most of England. It is a school that does not have the widest spectrum of ability; only 9% of the students are considered to be 'high achievers' on intake.

In writing this story of the CP in Thanet it is important to look at the context of King Ethelbert School. In 2009, when Paul Luxmoore, the Executive Headteacher of King Ethelbert, and I joined the school, the examination results (GSCEs) at aged16 were very poor: only 14% of students in a year group achieved grades of A*–C in five subjects, including English and maths. The Secretary of State for Education at the time initiated what was known as the National Challenge programme whereby all schools were directed to ensure 30% or more students achieved grades A*–C in five subjects, including English and maths. We had a job to do to improve academic performance, but our job was made more difficult by the non-selective nature of our school and the perceptions of a significant proportion of our community. A proportion of families believed that the aspirations of the students should be kept to a minimum because of the high level of unemployment in the area. Although I have worked in the eastern part of Kent for over 20 years, I was astounded when I heard parents tell me I was wrong to have aspirations for our young people. "There are no jobs here, what is the point?", "What will he/she do with 5 A*-C grades?" were lines I heard depressingly often.

King Ethelbert was a school for students aged 11 to 16. We had no Sixth Form (students aged 16–18) back in 2009, and although this was an aspiration for the school, we had other work to do before this could become a focus. By 2012 our GCSE results were much better and it was time to move everything up a gear and establish a King Ethelbert Sixth Form. Our exam results were better but had plateaued, and students had to leave our school at the age of 16 to study at a different institution. Although local provision for post-16 study for our students was good, there is no doubt that having a Sixth Form in a school makes a significant difference to the hopes and aspirations of students lower down the school who aspire to be like the older students. Also a relatively short post-16 study programme of two years meant that a move to another establishment led to students taking time to settle in socially, which could adversely affect the results they achieved 18 months later.

Finding the right programme

But what to offer at our new Sixth Form? In 2009, King Ethelbert became federated with a local grammar school, Dane Court, which offered the DP in its Sixth Form. Paul Luxmoore was the head teacher there before he became King Ethelbert's Executive Headteacher and had always been a keen advocate of an IB education. Initially Dane Court offered both A Levels and the DP but Paul found that difficult to justify: "I felt the DP was a much better programme, yet I'd have to promote both routes, equally, to students and parents". In 2012 he made the decision to offer only the DP in Dane Court Sixth Form; this was a brave decision given that A Levels was the known entity for post-16 academic provision across the whole of England. But the DP offers breadth – significant, life-changing breadth – not only in the number of subjects the students have to take but also through the DP core (Theory of Knowledge; Creativity, Activity, Service; the Extended Essay) which gives the students the skills needed for life.

The stalling point for me when considering what to offer post-16, as an alternative to A Levels at King Ethelbert School, was the wholly academic nature and rigour of the DP, including the compulsory language element with which so many of the students at our school would struggle. I believe fervently in vocational and academic learning being natural bedfellows that can lead to the best education for students up to the age of 18. At King Ethelbert we have always delivered academic GCSEs alongside vocational options pre-16. We want our young people to be educated academically – all students can access academic qualifications to a fairly significant level – but still have the study ethic and skills that vocational options offer. Vocational qualifications create learners who have to plan, prepare, refine, practise, think and apply; who does not want these skills in any work force or community?

The CP at King Ethelbert

At King Ethelbert we wanted a Sixth Form and a programme that was rigorous and challenging for our students but also had those key elements of learning and skill-development provided by a combination of academic and vocational education. When the CP landed in our lap, it was one of those rare moments where everything comes together, providing a golden opportunity for the school.

The academic rigour of the DP courses stretches and challenges the students in the same way as A Levels, but there is so much more to the CP than that. The career-related study element of the CP can come from a whole host of practical, applied, vocational subjects. In addition the programme offers those skills that are absolutely necessary for both university study and future employment.

Schools in England are set targets and numerical thresholds for students to achieve at key stages of their education, but what happens next? Although many students go to university, the retention rate is variable and not always as good as it should be; some students find the independent study required of them at university simply unmanageable. At the same time, there are many students who go to university and graduate but may not necessarily acquire the skills required for employment. Of course young people acquire these skills as they mature, but it can be a steep and sometimes painful learning curve. Further attainment and personal achievement could be achieved if young people were taught these skills as part of their post-16 education. The CP allows us to do just that. King Ethelbert was one of the Kent schools in a partnership pilot to explore whether DP courses could be delivered in a school that had not yet been authorised to teach the DP, but which would be supported by an authorised experienced DP school. We needed something that suited our school and the CP was just coming into fruition; it was perfect.

Particular elements of the CP have had a profound impact on the school and the students. What follows is a brief description and discussion of these elements.

Learning a language

I remember debates in the year preceding our first intake of CP students about the place of language learning in the CP. All IB students must study a second or additional language and I was adamant that language learning should feature heavily in the CP at King Ethelbert. However, the DP examines additional languages: all DP students must take a second or additional language course and be examined in it in order to achieve the diploma. The IB decided not to follow this path with the CP, but still wanted schools to teach an additional language or languages as part of the programme – teach, immerse the students, excite, stimulate and motivate – but <u>not</u> examine them.

The IB is committed to very high standards, but it treats teachers and head teachers as professionals and it gives credence to plain common sense. What freedom this approach to language learning opened up for us: allowing schools to use their professional judgement as to how additional languages would be delivered across the Sixth Form. We could include an additional language in the Sixth Form for the students to enjoy without the pressures of an examination at the end. Like many non-selective schools in Kent we had struggled for many years to find language teachers. Many of our students at the lower end of the ability spectrum struggled with an additional language, but there was more to it than this. Parents were not convinced of the importance of learning foreign or second languages and, coupled with a distinct lack of modern foreign language teachers in the market, additional languages in schools are becoming more and more scarce.

So what did we do? We asked our staff if anyone wanted to learn an additional language alongside our students; it would be fun, exciting, relevant but without the pressure to achieve prescribed targets. One of our Physical Education teachers had been to Italy the summer before and had already told me how frustrating he found it that he had such limited skills in Italian. So our CP students learnt Italian alongside him and it was very successful. It became a co-teaching experience between teacher and student that was exciting; everyone finished the course, thrilled that they knew so much, with many of our young people eager to go on and learn more foreign languages. "Because we can and because it is fun", was the cry from one student. They learnt the language and so much more: they studied the history of Italy, explored the culture, cooked the food, joined up in a partnership with an Italian school and made a film – they even insisted that I introduce the film in Italian. We got involved with a local language school where foreign students come over to learn English, and we held discos and reciprocal events so that many of our students became firm friends with their Italian counterparts. By releasing the school and the students from the pressure of a formal examination they became excited by learning about other countries and, suddenly, parochial Thanet got so much bigger. In an after-note to this, may I say that not only did the students became excited about languages but their parents and, thus, the community did too. On our next advertisement for a modern foreign languages teacher we got an application from someone who has, over the last three years, revolutionised language learning at our school. Spanish is now the most popular option for our students when they choose subjects at the age of 14, and we have also introduced a Spanish examined option as a DP course.

Acquiring important skills

In the CP core, the Personal and Professional Skills (PPS) course ensures that students are taught the skills to know where and how to find the information they need to fill the gaps in their knowledge. As a head teacher, one of the sources I rely on is my own experience of schooling and the resolve to make it better for future generations. For example, when studying for my A Levels at school, I could have quoted huge chunks of Shakespeare's 'Hamlet', and I knew the intricacies of the workings of a kidney inside out. However, on my first day at university I was given an essay title: 'Fool said my muse to me, look into my eyes and write'. I had two weeks to track the source, read appropriate poems and write a two thousand word essay. I panicked but I had to get on with it. The panic of not knowing how to approach that task has never left me. Our students today need knowledge but, more importantly, they need the skills to access that knowledge and to know what to do with it. The PPS course in the CP enables that to happen. One of the great joys of my job is walking into our Sixth Form area and seeing King Ethelbert students studying and behaving like undergraduates. True, they have the magic of technology which has opened up possibilities never envisaged in the early 1980s, but they can also use reference books, make telephone calls, find references and resources, work as a team to solve a problem and they have confidence as learners that makes me proud and certain that if they go to university they will not panic, they will not be overwhelmed, and they will succeed in what they need to do.

Learning through service

The service learning element of the CP core provides the same exciting opportunities as the other parts (Personal and Professional Skills; Language Development; the Reflective Project) and, as the name suggests, has an impact not only on the school community but also on the wider community of Thanet. This element again has the broadest base from which schools can make their own choice about how it is delivered, the caveat being that it should make some significant difference not only to the students, but also to the community.

Our first cohort of 10 CP students at King Ethelbert and, therefore, the first Sixth Form students ever, decided to work as a whole group to plan and execute the main event for the 75th Anniversary of our school opening. They were given £2,000 and told: 'Do it!'. It was entirely up to them to decide what form it should take, how many people to invite to the affair, and when it should take place. There were the inevitable debates about when to hold it, how much food to buy, how to source the cheapest deals on cutlery and deciding what would make a great table decoration, not to mention the question of what entertainment to have.

I have never seen a learning curve quite so steep for our students. Of course there were the inevitable teamwork issues, and there was a strong sense of discovery when it was revealed that two of the team had not yet managed to complete the task assigned to them. There were rows, tears, the slamming of doors and a palpable sense of frustration, both with other members of the team, and with plans having to be altered to fit in with the limited budget. The skills learnt during that period are too vast to list, but the sense of responsibility, pride and achievement the students experienced when the event finally took place and was deemed a great success was enormous. This was learning that was way beyond the scope of the normal school curriculum and there was no opt-out for anyone because this was part of their CP!

Since that initial event there have been other notable and important community events planned and delivered by groups of our Sixth Form students. One event worth mentioning was the local business fair organised by the students and held in the nearby community hall just before Christmas. It was an inspired choice by the students. Local businesses had an authentic and important opportunity to work with the students at their local school, and also an opportunity to promote themselves in a way that no advertisement in the local paper could do. Since that first fair it has been run again by the networks of the local businesses formed by King Ethelbert students.

Building support for the CP

People who are thinking of implementing the CP at their own schools often ask me how I persuaded students, parents and staff to adopt this hitherto unknown programme. It was, arguably, easier for us than for those schools who traditionally ran A Level courses. Students who were staying on at King Ethelbert had no choice: the CP was the only programme we were offering. Students are brave and courageous but they also trust their school to set them on the right paths and we, as a leadership team, were convinced about the CP. Our parents also show trust in our leadership and are generally happy with whatever course or programme we decide to implement. Of course, since the first cohort, we have had huge success with the CP and word of mouth is one of the most powerful tools for any school. The IB organisation has been very good at marketing the CP and we have worked hard with our local higher education establishments to promote what we knew would be a success. Canterbury Christ Church University was particularly helpful and made a formal contract with us, stating that any student who studied the CP would be guaranteed an interview or a place on their desired course if the number of UCAS points were attained.

One of the strengths of the CP is that while the three parts of the programme: DP courses; the CP core; the career-related study, together provide powerful learning opportunities for the individual student, certain elements of the programme are also courses that universities already recognise. The career-related part of the programme is, in the case of King Ethelbert, a BTEC Level 3 which is a course that has been taken by many students for many years in post-16 establishments as a route to university. The certificate of a BTEC vocational course is the equivalent of 2 A Levels, and the extended certificate is the equivalent of 3 A Levels. In that way the gamble of an unknown programme, the CP, becomes far less risky and universities across the country recognise these qualifications as established routes for undergraduate courses. All our students take the full CP and all our students pass the full CP, but there is comfort in the fact that BTEC Level 3 courses are already widely established and recognised.

The governors of King Ethelbert have always been supportive: Dane Court, our federated grammar school, already ran the DP. I remember a thrilling moment when we asked four of our CP students to talk to our governors about their learning on the CP. They did not talk of the subject knowledge they had acquired, they talked about how they learnt, in what ways they had researched, how they applied knowledge and, most importantly of all, the connections they could make between all the elements of the programme. I would argue that the epitome of outstanding education is the ability of the students to make connections, and the CP quite simply makes them do this.

Teaching staff at UK schools are highly professional and committed, but can be wary of yet another educational initiative. However, I showed the teachers at King Ethelbert the attributes of the IB Learner Profile that threads through all components of the CP. How would any teacher not see that we all want to create students who inquire, are resilient, who are independent and internationally minded? The CP, and the IB Learner Profile, have had an impact on teaching across the whole of our school, not just in our Sixth Form. Teachers, without having to be asked, saw huge value in the Learner Profile attributes and began threading them through their schemes of work in all years. This year we have developed the Learner Profile student of the week in our year 7 (11 years old) curriculum so that we have, for example, the most resilient student of the week. When people talk about Sixth Form students having an impact on the rest of the school it is so much more at King Ethelbert than having excellent role models and exemplary senior prefects. It is the Sixth Form curriculum and the skills of being a great learner that are impacting every aspect of our school.

King Ethelbert's CP graduates

I cannot write this chapter without writing about the successes of King Ethelbert's CP graduates. We have had 63 students study for and complete the CP. Some of them have gone to our local universities to study subjects such as midwifery, film and media, or accountancy and economics. Others have gone further afield: one student went to Falmouth in Cornwall, to study art and received a prize in his first year for photography. One student went to Edinburgh to study public relations – a student who had never travelled further than London before! Another student was accepted on a forensics course at Reading University which is notoriously difficult to get on to. One of our girls achieved a Grade 7 in DP maths standard level this year and is now reading physics at Nottingham University. Two thirds of the students who have gone to university are the first generation in their families to do so. Other students have taken up apprenticeships and, if they are local, I am always hearing how good they are: "A credit to your school", because they have the skills that many others do not learn until later on in life. They can problem solve, give a presentation, be confident, and know where to look for answers. I would willingly offer employment to all of these students. Indeed one of our first CP students has come home to Thanet after her successful university years to become a teacher, training at King Ethelbert, her old school. I remember a wonderful moment when one of our students was on his mobile phone in the common room making the best deal he could in order to be taken on as a stock broker. It was his ambition and he achieved it. Another student told me that university was "my second choice", and I marvelled at the way our students were able to take their futures into their own hands.

"The CP got us to aspire to things we never thought we could be capable of – it has changed my whole family for the better" (Graduate 2014).

"The CP made me brave, allowed me to take risks and has made me aware that I am so much better than average" (Graduate 2015).

The sentiments of these two students sum up what we all feel at King Ethelbert.

And so, finally, back to Rachel, who knocked on my door to tell me of her acceptance at university. As I said, she encapsulates the story of King Ethelbert's school. Rachel started at King Ethelbert seven years ago as a student who was considered to be, at the age of 11, a low attainer. She had always been a delightful child. She was shy, unsure of herself, rather fearful of what the future might offer, although her GCSE grades were good enough for her to get a place in our Sixth Form and she started to blossom. My word, how she bloomed in the Sixth Form! Here she was, seven years later, telling me that she had achieved a place at university.

We all know that good education changes lives. I have seen many, many students' lives transformed through their study of the CP. This year we had 118 students interviewed for a place to study the CP at King Ethelbert. The word is spreading, and quite rightly, because this is education at its absolute best.

The future of the CP at King Ethelbert

So what does the future hold for the CP at King Ethelbert School and across Kent? As always in education there are challenges to be faced and things that, collectively, we have to put in place. Kent, as a county, has become very enthusiastic about the CP, seeing the positive benefits it has heralded both at King Ethelbert and in the other pilot schools across the area. The backing of Kent County Council is very important and promising conversations are being held at school level and at larger conferences; we at King Ethelbert will, of course, be spreading the word. 20 other schools locally have signed up for the accelerated route to CP authorisation. They have set up a network of head teachers so that good practice can be shared, and advice and help given, in order that the CP can be implemented as quickly as possible in those schools for the benefit of all of the young people in the county.

The administrative processes of the IB can be onerous and the documentations we had to complete to achieve IB World School authorisation is time consuming. This is understandable given the standards the IB aims to maintain, but if our schools can work together to share the administrative processes this makes the whole journey of becoming an IB World School far less daunting.The visit from IB officers and the standards required for programme delivery are a very good thing and help to fine tune the way the CP is delivered in each individual school. Although we have been frustrated with the administration we have had nothing but support, advice and critical friendship from the IB organisation.

Funding is obviously a challenge to us all. UK schools are facing uncertain times financially, for many reasons. The IB insists on training for all: as a head teacher, I had to attend a two-day training event, four years after we started implementing the CP, to ensure we could become an IB World School. Initially I was quite critical about this requirement, but the training was excellent and I learnt a lot; it certainly helped us, as a school, to refine our implementation of the CP and gave us many ideas on how we could move things forward across all year groups in the school. But implementing an IB programme is expensive for state-funded schools and this is a significant concern to many would-be IB schools in the UK. However, the more schools in an area that take on the CP the more they can work together and share. We have been delighted with some of the cluster training we have received locally – workshops for a group or cluster of CP schools located geographically in the same area. Not only have the training days been good for our staff and provided a great networking opportunity, they have also been affordable.

I continue to worry about the academic versus vocational debate that still rages on in the UK. Only recently a government strategic paper was produced that hit the educational headlines, advocating the splitting of academic and vocational qualifications once and for all, for all students over the age of 16. The general tenor of the paper was that academic qualifications would remain in schools whilst vocational qualifications, post-16, would become the sole responsibility of further education or tertiary colleges. It is hard to see the benefit of channelling students into one pathway or another at the age of 16, as proposed by this government paper, and I fear it would be the death knell for the CP in schools in England. So, there are potential fights to be had, money to be found and administration to be done, but I remain optimistic.

Of course we cannot predict the exact nature of any future challenges, I do know that any school I lead will have an IB education at the centre of it and I will continue to promote the life-changing effects the CP has had and continues to have at King Ethelbert. We have 70 new first year CP students, making the total number in our Sixth Form studying the CP well over 100. I know these students have a very bright future ahead. Word is spreading and now people in Thanet are talking about the CP, what it is and the impact it is having on our young people in this complex coastal community. The CP quite simply can change lives and change communities, and that makes the future very exciting indeed.

Chapter 11

The Career-related Programme as a pathway to university for students of the creative arts in Queensland, Australia

John Carozza

The context

The Queensland Academy for Creative Industries (QACI) is one of three purpose-built academies, established by Education Queensland, Australia, in 2007 and 2008. Each academy is housed on a separate campus but under the same Queensland Academies banner. The academies were designed as publicly funded government schools, to cater for students of high academic ability, who would all complete the IB Diploma Programme (DP) as their Senior High schooling pathway, instead of the Queensland School's Certificate that the majority of the Queensland high schools were completing.

This was at a point when the Australian National Curriculum had not been embraced in Queensland, yet Education Queensland made the innovative move of creating an educational pathway for students who were some of the state's best and brightest students. QACI's aim is to provide a point of difference in the educational market through an enriched secondary education programme, encompassing the DP, university experience, industry experience and, where appropriate, accelerated pathways for our state's students. It is essentially about encouraging creative capital.

Each academy has selective entry requirements in their specialist fields. QACI has an entry point through the students' DP group 6 subjects (visual arts, film, theatre and music); these are known as their *Signature Creative Identity*. QACI became the first DP school in the world where students were able to complete two group 6 subjects; in a standard Diploma Programme, students can only study one of the group 6 arts subjects to achieve a diploma. Over the first few years of the QACI's development, it became evident that DP group 6 students were nothing if not unique in their educational outlook and, when gathered together, became an artistic student think tank, a collective that proved to be both challenging and exciting for the teaching staff. It is worth noting that all of the teachers for the DP group 6 courses are practising artists in their own right. Many of the students had a clear artistic pathway mapped out in their heads, and already knew which area of the arts world they wanted to enter as well as, in many cases, which university they wished to attend.

Introducing the Career-related Programme (CP) at QACI

The founding principal of QACI (affectionately pronounced '*Quacky*' by the staff and students) began to formulate a way to accommodate the high ability students the academy was designed to cater for yet who, in many cases, were struggling with the combination of their artistic practice and the rigour and volume of the DP. The students were achieving at a very high level across the whole spectrum of DP subjects, yet already knew which artistic pathway they wanted to follow.

Mr John Jose, the principal of QACI from 2007 to 2014, researched the CP as an opportunity for the students not to do a less rigorous programme, but to complete an alternative programme in their signature areas of study. QACI was housed in an urban village, in a university precinct, and it established links with the neighbouring university from the beginning of its existence. In fact, a virtual feeder system had developed with many students gaining admission to this university. Therefore Jose felt it would be possible to implement the CP as a university pathway, with university studies in the chosen arts being the career-related studies element of the CP. The university in question, Queensland University of Technology (QUT), had already acknowledged the quality of our students' coursework and our teaching staff, evidenced by having QACI staff guest lecture at their institution each year. I was brought in on a sessional basis to teach in the World Cinema and Australian Cinema courses. As an interesting side note, the lecture I give regularly on particular films, for first, second and third year university students, is one I use with my DP Year 11 and Year 12 film classes. This is an example of the level at which our students are working.

The plan was to offer the CP as a high-end academic option for our high achieving film students who already knew they would be pursuing studies in the creative industries at QUT. The university course would be the career-related study component of the CP and it would mean that they would attend lectures in QUT's Creative Industries' first year subjects, alongside university students, completing the set tasks and interacting on practical projects. They would also complete four DP courses at QACI as part of their CP. The first and second cohorts of CP students were selected from the DP film cohort, as a controlled sample. Being a foundation teacher and Head of Group 6 (the exotically titled Head of Creative Signature Identity), I was also the DP film teacher for the students in question, which allowed for a smoother transition and one-on-one contact, along with my university contact already being established.

The students' career-related study takes place at the partner university, QUT, where CP students attend a two-hour lecture, plus a one-hour tutorial per week. They take the following courses: Introduction to Entertainment; the Movie, TV & New Media Business; Narrative Production and Introduction to Scriptwriting. As film students, the topic that was explored as an ethical issue in their career-related study – a requirement of the CP – was in relation to the visual and textual representations in the art form and media form of their study.

What drives the CP at QACI?

The CP has the potential to expand the scope of learning beyond what is possible in the DP and to be "the mouse that roared'. QACI implemented the CP in 2013, with the first cohort of students selected from the DP film course. It provided the framework for the academy to build a programme around its most outstanding academic and artistic students. The students themselves felt freed up in terms of what they were studying to develop their passion, in this instance film studies, within the CP framework. One of the goals of building an educational paradigm around these chosen students was to build experiential and deeper understanding in the cohort, as though it was virtually a school-based honours programme. These students attended university lectures and tutorials and comfortably slotted into the environment. The university partners were very impressed with their attitude and the way they carried themselves as academics.

The Personal and Professional Skills (PPS) component of the CP was built around the subject from which the students were drawn. For the first wave of students, the PPS course was strongly flavoured by their study of film wherever possible. The sub-units that existed within the DP Film course allowed students to explore key concepts that fitted well within the PPS course: Metaphor, Metamorphosis and Transformation, Social Awareness and Being Human.

The undoubted attraction of DP courses lies in their academic rigour, depth of knowledge, global values and the broad cross-section of rich subject areas that can be tapped into by students and teachers, and in the intellectual stimulus and the way they prepare students to be autonomous learners and creative problem solvers. The strength of the CP, within this established academic scaffold, is its people-friendly interface that can be customised to the students' personal learning experiences, expectations and abilities, as well as a way of transitioning students between the real world and higher education.

By establishing the CP alongside the DP, the IB has allowed educators to create a bespoke educational pathway for its students who have identifiable and unique needs, not to mention meeting parental expectations. This could be considered to be a masterstroke by the IB. Using the CP to build a programme of study around the chosen art form enables students to reach a deeper level of skill, knowledge and understanding than they were able to reach in the time frames allocated to DP group 6 subjects. In terms of students of film, the academy was able to build in existential and artistic thinking exercises around cinema, and conceptual scaffolds from cinema from around the world, whilst maintaining the ideology of the QACI artistic model. This ideology was, and still is, the exploration and self-reflection as to what it means to be human, the human condition and how one fits within the world.

Central to this ideology, the PPS component was purposefully designed to cater for students who were firstly, highly academic and capable and, secondly, creative film students. PPS became an extension of their film course at the university, of their DP Film course and an important way of developing the attributes of the IB Learner Profile.

The QACI vision: building the CP

QACI saw the CP as combining elements that were a very good fit with its students: they could maintain their academic schooling through the four academically rigorous DP courses; they could expand their creative specialisation in career and artistic areas; and they could maintain a global outlook through the international nature of an IB education, supported by the philosophy of QACI. It was decided that the DP subjects would be chosen from Studies in Language and Literature (group 1), Language Acquisition (group 2), Individuals and Societies (group 3) and Arts (group 6) and the career-related pathway consisted of four prescribed arts-based university subjects studied over the two years of the CP.

The entry requirements for the CP at QACI are demanding: students have to attain a grade A for their pre-IB studies, (the foundation year at QACI) in their career-related subject, for example, film, visual arts, or design; maintain a grade B average or better in academic results for their other subjects; display a high level of work ethic, persistence and independent study; and demonstrate an understanding of, and alignment with, the stated outcomes of the CP model at QACI in their interview.

Initially two university partners were approached to be part of the CP at QACI. Both were keen once negotiations were underway, although in the end, one of these universities chose to give our CP film student cohorts advanced credit if they successfully competed the programme, whilst the other took on the students under a negotiated Memorandum of Agreement, ensuring them direct entry and advanced credit for four Creative Industries subjects. There is an interesting irony to the universities examining our DP group 6 courses and being aware of our student's level of work and work ethic which I will return to later.

The CP allowed us to create a specific career-related pathway for our high achieving students that was giving them, in reality, a very intensive learning experience of film studies whilst at the same time guaranteeing them entry and advanced credit into the university they were intending to enter on completion of the programme.

The Reflective Project

Three of the CP core components – PPS, Language Development and Service Learning – were implemented in a customised way, as intended by the IB. The externally moderated assessment component, the Reflective Project, drew upon the specific and honed skill sets of the particular cohorts of students. In year 1 of the CP (a cohort of four students), the students were focused on documentary film; they were skilled in editing and production processes and scored highly on the formative and summative assessment tasks of their DP courses. By allowing students to focus on a socio-cultural-political topic to which they could feel a personal and artistic connection, they were able to invest in the task and create a ten-minute micro–documentary that allowed both an illustration of their creative process and their deconstruction of a topic.

For example, by constructing a documentary from topics such as the *'The presence and representation of women on Australian television'* or *'The Australian media's responsibility in creating then demolishing sports stars'*, students were presented with a need to solve a problem creatively, liaise with the public and media outlets, research, film, edit and produce production documents to support their topic. The documentaries they created complemented their DP and university film courses and also became a piece for their digital artistic portfolio.

These films were completed under guidance and direction from the CP coordinator, in this case myself. What became evident early in their work on the Reflective Project was that the intensity of constant one-on-one contact between teacher and student was providing the students with a deeper knowledge of the topic they were preparing, and increasing the research skills and the editing process. This finding is not a surprise, but it reinforces the theory that high-achieving students are able to go to an even higher level when they are given the opportunity to focus academically on a strength and have specific teacher guidance. Mainstream education often places these students as autonomous learners, not needing as much contact, with the teacher sharing time with those who are struggling. By removing this limitation to contact there was a huge leap in the quality of the work of the students, already at a very high level. It gave strength to the value QACI had placed in its founding beliefs that a DP grade 7 is not the highest grade you can attain. It may be numerically, but as an artist there is so much more you can achieve.

Personal and Professional Skills

For QACI the essence of the CP's PPS course was in how it was possible to create a learning workflow specifically designed for film students who were high achieving, whilst embedding the traditional learning areas. The course outline and workflow, shown in table 1, illustrate the way I approached the PPS content for year1 CP film students. It should be noted that the Reflective Project runs parallel to the PPS course.

PPS Course Unit	Content
Introduction to PPS	• What is PPS? • Why PPS matters. • The IB Learner Profile • What are the goals and requirements of the CP?
Embed: intercultural understanding; thinking and communication; personal development Section (a) • Ethical thinking /morality • Critical thinking • Creative thinking • Problem thinking • Lateral thinking	*The Learning Model : what sort of learner are you?* • Multiple intelligences • Right vs. left brain • Does genius exist? Students examine the following areas: • What are ethics? • What are their own values? • What are cultural values? • What are world values/beliefs? • What are the skills needed? • When would being a critical thinker be of use? • Creativity • Creativity activities • Evaluate each activity • How can we measure creativity? • Brainstorming • Evaluate the difference between critical and creative thinking • Problem solving activities
Section (b) • Discovering the types of thinking. Which do I use the most?	• History of neurological study • Brain chemistry • Changing and developing learning skills
Section (c) • Why are the different types of thinking important? • What is critical thinking? • What is creative thinking? Section (d) • How does the brain work? • Brain chemistry and developing learning patterns • Unlearning behaviours • Changing opinions • Influencing opinions	• Significant philosophers of the past and contemporary philosophical thinkers. • What is a philosophical and ethical approach to creating documentary? • Is impartiality possible?

Table 1: Sample PPS outline year 1

Reflections on implementing the CP

Getting the message right

After guiding two cohorts of students through the CP, I believe a school wishing to establish the CP as a parallel programme of study, alongside the DP, could benefit from considering the following suggestions. Firstly, create a detailed plan that is clear for all stake-holders, so that the students in the course, the teachers, the school administration, the parents and the career-related studies' providers all have the same story to tell and see why everything is happening as it is. Secondly, the story should be refined so that everyone is aware that by following this programme, structured in this particular way and filled with this content, including the career-related pathway, the students will be able to head in a clear and certain direction after they complete their CP studies, with advanced skills and standing. I think it is also vital that the school, and in particular the teachers who are working in this programme, have a very clear understanding of what the three major components of the programme are and understand the potential that can be realised with each of these.

Developing an integrated programme of study

The CP at QACI has been developed so that it is a very high-end academic strand of the IB, essentially the equivalent of an honours course in film studies within the school, with the students also attending university lectures as an integral part of the programme. The PPS course is a philosophical and existential exploration of thinking, being human and how all of these ideas can be seen through the many varieties of film genre and film making style. On top of their study of film it provides a completely immersive line of study. The Reflective Project and Service Learning projects are also flavoured this way.

The CP proved to be a success for the students who undertook it, primarily by providing them with a career-related pathway that was their goal for their tertiary studies. But it also strengthened film studies at QACI, through the development of the PPS component. The conceptual underpinning of what it means to be human is fundamental to the QACI ethos, particularly in film studies, so through the opportunity to elaborate this existential scaffold in PPS, the CP was given a spine around which to build extended discussion and stimuli.

An example for this was the time spent on the unit of *Trans-humanism*, where through cinematic artists and cinematic themes, the exploration of moral, ethical and socio-political issues could be placed central to extended areas of student study. Take for instance, using *The Matrix* (dir. Wachowski et al, 1999) as a stimulus for the examination of personal consciousness and reality. This is a film in use with many high school film and TV, media and even English classes as well as DP theory of knowledge classes. An obvious entry point but, through a bespoke PPS course, the students were able to delve deeper into the idea of personal reality and human frailty and strength that, through a detailed deconstruction of the amazing *La rivière du hibou (An Occurrence at Owl Creek Bridge,* dir. Enrico, 1962) they may never have had the chance to have done in the limited time frame of an open film course. *La rivière du hibou*, is a short story written by Ambrose Bierce, first published by the San Francisco examiner in 1890 and then turned into a Cannes and Academy award winning short film in 1964. It aired on US television as an episode of The Twilight Zone, the first film in fact shown as a stand-alone episode and one that has formed the template for many films and stories of science fiction and fantasy.

To build this study into the PPS component was one of the great benefits of the CP. Having it populated by high achieving film students, we were able to go beyond the initial ideas and, through examination of more challenging films, genuinely take students into deeper, extended learning. *La rivière du hibou* was complemented by study of *The Matrix* and the principles of quantum mechanics, *Dark City* (dir. Proyas,1998) and the contemplation of personal reality: how we know what we know.

Personal and Professional Skills: a sample assessment task

An Occurrence at Owl Creek Bridge dir. Robert Enrico (1962) from "*La rivière du hibou*", based on the short story by Ambrose Bierce (Part 2 of a Civil War Trilogy by Robert Enrico).

After viewing the film and exploring the conceptual ideas that have been studied in class, such as:

(a) Time viewed as a personal perception of reality

(b) What it means to be human

(c) Existentialism and philosophical concepts

(d) Quantum mechanics

and in looking at this short film as a piece of cinema :

(a) Narratively

(b) Symbolically

(c) Allegorically

(d) Cinematically

explain how the film-maker has created a piece of art that brings together a questioning of what is reality and what is imagination, and how we, as viewers, are asked to examine his work.

Where to next?

Earlier I mentioned there was an irony to the university partners having a close look at our CP and DP course designs. Our CP students are high achieving film students and were able to demonstrate in their university courses how well read and accomplished they were. This partnership arrangement also contributed to QUT, where the students were attending first year courses as their career-related studies. For the students studying three of QACI's DP group 6 subjects: film, theatre and visual arts, QUT offered advanced credit for two of the first year subjects in Creative Industries. This meant that a student who passed the DP film and visual arts courses, for example, would receive four advanced university credits in their course of study at the university, the equivalent of the advanced credits for the whole of the CP. This, while well intentioned, removed a strong incentive for students to study the whole CP. So, one of the incentives for our future cohorts to be part of the CP, was now a given in terms of advanced credit. After discussion with QUT, we decided to pause the CP, to re-evaluate it over the next few years. This is the process that is taking place at the time of writing.

Does this mean the CP is no longer needed at QACI? Not at all. Though in its original form it is. The process will need to evolve in close collaboration with the university partners for a new agreement and for our next stage of development of the CP. It appears, in some ways, that we were a victim of our own success in terms of setting out with a goal to establish a school for the gifted, artistic student who needs a scholastic challenge and also needs to be around like-minded peers and teachers. The universities were, and are still, very keen to have our students attend, hence the advanced credit they are offering. Our closest university partner, QUT, has commented that it recognises our students by the way they approach their work and their research, and how they submit high quality work on time. Yet where this leaves our options to develop the CP is our challenge at present.

I foresee the area of design, particularly industrial and environmental design, being a focus for us in the near future, along with fashion and interior design. These courses are running at QUT and are where a number of our students attend post-QACI. The issue for us is being housed within the framework of our state education system, whilst being a totally IB World School. This may not appear at first glance a problem but, in a traditional education system such as ours, we have been under constant scrutiny since we opened. There has been professional and political comment and observation of our institution, our results and our product since day one. We have always been in some ways a square peg in a round hole, particularly being an arts-focused institution. Imagine thinking artistically creative students could be as smart as those who excel at mathematics or chemistry? Imagine a future where the doctors and engineers of your city or country have creative problem-solving skills and artistic sensibilities? This is the goal of our school and it is very difficult for more cynical observers to come to grips with this concept. The CP may be a way for us to reimagine what we are planning. It will take collaborations that will be as brave as they are new.

The CP is a programme with remarkable potential for students of all sorts of achievement levels, particularly if it is promoted and designed to be a parallel programme to the DP, not a lesser version. It allows a school to design and develop a programme to complement a particular path of study and embody the IB Leaner Profile in so doing. These are its strengths and the reasons I would suggest schools look closely at the CP as a viable and exciting option for their students.

References

Enrico, R. *et al* (1962): *La rivière du hibou/An occurrence at Owl Creek Bridge*. France: Filmartic.

Proyas, A. (1998): *Dark City*. Los Angeles, California: New Line Home Video.

Wachowski L., Reeves, K., Fishburne, L. and Moss, C. A. (1999): *The Matrix*. Burbank, California: Warner Home Video.

Part C

The Career-related Programme in an international context

Chapter 12

The Career-related Programme at the International School of Geneva

Conan de Wilde

In 2011, thanks to a grant from the Setton Foundation, I began researching how the International School of Geneva (Ecole Internationale de Genève, known as Ecolint) could expand its educational offering for the final two years of secondary school. This chapter is the reflections of one curriculum coordinator on how one of the oldest and largest international school in the world sought to implement a meaningful IB Career-related Programme (CP) at one of its campuses, the Campus des Nations. The story starts with the research and implementation phase and ends with the graduation of our first cohort of students. While no two schools are the same, some of our experiences during this journey will resonate with other schools who have implemented the CP.

I am writing this chapter for the same reason that I wanted to be involved with the CP in the first place. The CP is desperately needed by many students around the world. In bridging the gap between academic and vocational studies at secondary level and in international schools the CP is nothing short of revolutionary. It is my hope that by sharing Ecolint's experiences with the CP, other schools will feel confident that the programme can enrich their schools the way it has enriched ours.

2012 – 2013	Worked on and received IB authorisation to offer the CP
2013 – 2014	Eighteen students start the CP at the Campus des Nations of Ecolint
2014 – 2015	The first CP cohort graduates at Ecolint

Timeline for implementing the CP at Ecolint

The Ecolint context: diversity

Ecolint's diversity stretches well beyond the dreams of its founders who opened the school in 1924 for eight students. Currently Ecolint offers a multitude of academic courses through the medium of English and French. The programmes we offer include the IB Primary Years Programme (PYP), the IB Middle Years Programme (MYP), the UK based IGCSE (International General Certificate of Education, offered by Cambridge International Examinations), the school's own curriculum to build 21st century competences, the Maturité Suisse, the IB Diploma Programme (DP) and, of course, the CP – the subject of this chapter.

Ecolint is an open-access, private, not-for-profit educational foundation. The school is well known in the Geneva area for its Extended Support Programmes and learning support, and the school has attracted students who are extremely diverse in their academic profiles. The school also has a longstanding commitment to bilingual education and offers a wide range of subjects in French and English as well as English or French language acquisition support. Furthermore, mother tongue programmes support the national languages of many of the 140 nationalities held by its students. The linguistic and national diversity of Ecolint's students, coupled with our students' special education needs, presents a wide range of challenges in terms of helping them excel in the courses on offer while also preparing them to return for school or university in their countries of origin. Many of these challenges are well known by international schools around the world, but they remain an important part of the context into which the CP was introduced.

Today, Ecolint's size, spread out across three campuses and eight schools, provides us with the resources to allow us to cater, more than ever, for a community with wide-ranging needs. This celebration of diversity is part of the school's DNA. The recognition that there is not one right way to educate is central to what Ecolint is and Ecolint will continue, as mandated by article 4 of its charter (Ecolint, 2011), to educate "based on the principles of equality and solidarity among all peoples and of the equal value of all human beings without any distinction of nationality, race, sex, language or religion." Despite this genuine appreciation of diversity among its community, Ecolint's status as the oldest international school supports a traditional outlook with regards to curriculum. Ecolint teachers were involved in the birth of the DP in the 1960s. But Ecolint's historical role in the creation of the DP may have been one of the factors that inhibited the school from exploring and implementing alternative programmes. The recent creation of Extended Support Programmes, the growth of learning support departments and language support services, the creation of programmes for gifted students linked to the arts or STEM (science, technology, engineering and mathematics), and the introduction of the CP constitute major milestones for the school and are proof that Ecolint is able to take tangible action to support education for all members of its diverse student body.

Although Ecolint offered the kinds of courses and structures to support a linguistically diverse population and although the support for special educational needs was well established, there was one area in which Ecolint fell short of living out its promise of diversity. In 2010 Ecolint remained highly academic in its course offerings. Much energy was devoted to making sure that its diverse population graduated with the DP. A small number of students left the school after Year 12, a year before their peers were scheduled to sit their DP examinations; these students typically fulfilled the criteria for Ecolint's high school diploma and were, more often than not, bound for universities in the US. But these high school diploma students sat in the same classes as their DP peers, often took the same number of classes, and were assessed in the same way. Students who elected to follow DP courses only, rather than the full DP, had more flexibility in terms of their academic choices, but all the choices remained academic and those students were often sorely in need of the kind of metacognitive development which takes place in the core components (Theory of Knowledge; Creativity, Activity, Service; Extended Essay) of the DP – or the CP.

Every year graduates left Ecolint and went on to study courses in hotel schools, art colleges or technical colleges, taking degrees in domains such as sound engineering or set design. Every year groups of parents, students and teachers were left bewildered as to why certain students had to suffer through the strict confines of the DP's academic requirements when they had little interest in or use for their science course, or their mathematics course or some other subject that had been torturing them for two long years! Furthermore, these students sometimes felt further disadvantaged by not having had enough time to build up a portfolio in art, or get the basics of a hands-on approach to business, or by not having had sufficient experience in music studios. We claimed, as a school, that we were student-centred and yet, because the DP remained the gold standard of success, we couldn't adequately celebrate the diverse talents and aspirations of our students. If all students in a diverse community feel pushed to aspire to high marks in the DP, many students will inevitably feel frustrated, stunted in their growth and even alienated.

Searching for a solution

As a school, we recognised not only the changing demands of our students, but also the changing contexts of higher education and employment. We knew that high prestige vocational education was on the rise. Regular articles in educational journals and in the mainstream press alerted us all to this trend. Yet, despite our location in Switzerland, where vocational training has more prestige than in many countries, we were sceptical as to whether our international parent body could be convinced that a vocational option was good enough for their children. Another obstacle for us when considering the introduction of career-related qualifications was that they tended to be national or regional in their recognition, a factor which would dissuade our highly mobile student body from considering this type of study.

I began researching internationally-recognised vocational qualifications around the time when the IB was launching its first CP pilot schools. The IB was, and still is, the only organisation offering a programme of study for 16-19 year olds which is international in terms of the nature of the curriculum requirements (specifically with regards to the requirement for foreign language development) and international in terms of the scope of its recognition at universities around the world and by national bodies. Part of the CP involves the completion of recognised career-related studies, yet the IB has not yet been able to offer a range of specific vocational qualifications and, therefore, leaves the choice of career-related qualifications up to the school. It soon became clear that Pearson's BTEC (Business and Technology Educational Council) vocational qualifications had the greatest choice in terms of units of study and also had widespread international recognition by employers and providers of tertiary education. The BTEC (level 3) was clearly the most desirable qualification to fold into the CP at Ecolint. I spent over a year trying to obtain the authorisation to offer Swiss vocational qualifications to our students as their career-related component, but the Geneva cantonal department of education was unable to commit definitively to the framework proposed and the seeds we scattered at various levels of the Département d'Instruction Public bore no fruit. In the end, given that our first cohort had career and university aspirations in Australia, Papua New Guinea, Canada, the UK, the US, Switzerland, France, South Africa and Namibia, the combination of BTEC courses, DP courses and the innovative experiential learning of the CP almost certainly allowed students a wider range of choices of countries and universities than a Swiss vocational qualification would have permitted.

A solution that needs selling

Over the last six years I have met with a large number of CP coordinators, and their greatest challenge has been selling the programme. CP coordinators would often note the gap between their skill set and training, and the reality of setting up a successful CP programme. Over and over I heard: "I was trained as a teacher, but now my job is sales!" And it was true. The research stage, the authorisation to offer the CP and the implementation of the programme were enjoyable and relatively easy compared to the challenge of selling the CP to colleagues, board members, prospective parents, students and partners in industry. Not only do these exercises in marketing – creating brochures, speaking at events, meeting with individuals, pitching companies to forge relationships – take a lot of time, but there is a sense of uncertainty which I found bewildering. I would set aside several hours to answer emails from prospective parents and students and then meet with them, only to never hear from them again. That said, the excitement of finding students who would genuinely benefit from the programme was an undeniable pleasure.

Given our students and parent body, I felt that, in order to convince the school's governing board and parents that there was a place for vocational education in the school, we needed to make such education prestigious. I tried to point to patterns in national education systems. Sweden, Finland, Switzerland, Germany and Austria all have strong public vocational education programmes; Greece, Spain, Italy and Portugal typically don't. Better vocational education leads to more resilient economies and lower youth unemployment rates. The problem was that, although everyone seemed to agree that better, more widespread vocational education supports sustained economic growth, many parents still pushed their children towards academic, highly abstract qualifications. The strongest reason for this rush towards increasingly academic qualifications at the secondary school level may be social prestige. Even if plumbers can make a lot of money, that line of work is rarely thought of as prestigious – either among teenagers or their parents. But vocational education, I tried to argue, is also an inspiring way to access careers in aerospace engineering, in business, in a wide range of creative industries, in healthcare, and in hotel management. These are high-prestige fields because they are useful to society, they are well remunerated and they can provide career flexibility and high levels of job satisfaction.

Some parents and board members were also reluctant to associate education with careers for educational reasons not linked to prestige. Despite the many benefits of a focused vocational education for society, we know that academic education teaches students important skills too. I opined that we had a course which was internationally recognised, attached to a well-known educational brand and which also had academic kudos. In my conversations with parents they frequently associated academic courses with the ability to use language to analyse a wide range of situations and they felt that the well-rounded approach of an academic curriculum leads to superior communication skills. They were right. But, if vocational education is traditionally associated with resilience and resourcefulness, and academic approaches are thought of as strong in analysis and communication, the CP allowed us to marry these two approaches while benefiting, at the same time, from some degree of international recognition. The CP allowed us to present parents with the best of both worlds. There was no longer a need to choose between the joy of intellectual exploration for its own sake and the need to make one's way in the world. Furthermore, the CP framework gave us the flexibility to blend a specific mix of the academic and the applied, depending on the student's needs.

Unfortunately, I soon discovered that arguing the general benefits of a curriculum was not the best way to attract students to the CP! They (both students and parents) all had the same fear: would the CP close doors and limit student prospects? Vocational success stories on a national level did nothing to allay these fears. Citing examples of students' university admissions from other schools who had been piloting the CP was helpful in calming some of these fears, but it was not sufficient to attract them to register for the programme. What worked was listening to individual student interests and demonstrating that the CP could be tailored to those interests.

You want to become a fashion designer? How about DP Design Technology Higher Level, where you can learn about the design cycle? Or DP Art Higher Level, where you can focus on fashion drawing? What about English language and literature where you can study the language of advertising and aesthetics, and French, which will give you access to some great design schools in Switzerland and neighbouring France? We can support you doing some fashion-focused units in your BTEC classes and we can also develop your photography skills so that you can showcase your creations digitally. We will enable you to build a great portfolio and set some time aside for work placements.

Students who really want to be designers find it hard to resist doing more of what they love. Most parents were also convinced of the benefits of an education tailored to their child when they saw an adolescent with downcast eyes, and who was typically withdrawn, look up and engage with a conversation and make counter-proposals of their own. When you can close the meeting with an affirmation that they are a good student in all areas except mathematics and sciences – and they don't even need those DP courses to be a fashion designer – the student is delighted. Parents usually understand that a programme that showcases and then develops their child's strengths will open many more doors than a package in which many of the subjects are uninteresting to the student and which will highlight their academic failures day after day.

Bridging the gap between academic and career-related learning

Learning to apply subject knowledge to a career context is what quality career-related education is all about, and it remained our greatest challenge as we built and reviewed units of study, and as we sought to build ties with organisations such as PricewaterhouseCoopers (PwC), Procter and Gamble, local banks, photographers, graphic designers and marketing specialists. Students need to be taught how to apply academic knowledge to real world contexts, and it is here that academic education can benefit from the traditions of vocational education, a tradition that goes far beyond work experience, a tradition that remains rigorously focused on the context of the problem that needs solving.

From September 2013 the Ecolint Campus des Nations began teaching the CP, the first school in Switzerland to do so. Two career-related pathways were available: business, and art and design. Both areas of professional specialisation sought to prepare students for university studies, but we had our eyes set on the far horizon, and our ultimate goal was to prepare students to excel in the careers of their choice. Employers want skilful, knowledgeable, tenacious, and creative employees who show a knowledge of global concerns grounded in a solid ethical framework. This is exactly what the CP aims to deliver. That said, some of our students struggled with basic skills either because of diagnosed learning difficulties or because they had gaps in their schooling. This was sometimes accompanied by a crippling lack of motivation. For many students learning one skill well, such as touch-typing or film editing or poster design, was the breakthrough. Once they mastered a skill and received recognition for it, we had a more solid platform from which to access more complex communication, organisation and numeracy skills. Emphasising key principles helped us to develop the CP as a way to accommodate limited students and to stretch the very able. I continue to believe that it is essential to attract highly able students to the CP to maintain a dynamic and challenging classroom environment.

Providing students with choice

We constructed the requirements of the Ecolint CP curriculum based on the premise that if students can drop subjects they don't like and choose those they love, then they will be more passionate about their studies. Students can choose between two and four DP courses and they can take these at Higher or at Standard Level. Since students are more highly motivated by their chosen subjects they will work harder to acquire the academic knowledge and the analytical skills prized by that subject area. Thus the flexibility and the focus of the CP will help students excel. We also review our BTEC business units and art and design units annually, based on the interests of the cohort. Involving students in the construction of the curriculum is important as many of them have been made to feel like failures at school; their input can help us design the programme to meet their educational and personal needs.

Whilst choice has given students a say when constructing their course of study, once this is decided upon it is essential that teaching strategies and expectations are structured and clear. This clarity is especially important in terms of the transfer of knowledge from the theoretical realm to a practical application. For many students in secondary school the most difficult skill to master is knowing when to use knowledge from one practical application to solve a new problem. Students make the knowledge transfer more effectively when they feel that they are faced with a meaningful real-life context related to their chosen study in either business or art and design. In addition to this the BTEC criteria are very easy to interpret and they lend themselves to practical tasks. Business students might be asked, for example, to produce a cash flow statement for a local company which meets the International Accounting Standard; art and design students might be asked to use motion blur, differential focus, depth of field, and *bokeh* (a Japanese term for the way the lens renders out-of-focus points of light) in their location photography portfolios to help market a sporting event. Students might then be assessed on their ability to combine these techniques coherently with a range of technologies and recording media for ease of distribution. Because the BTEC has so many units to choose from, and there is a certain amount of overlap between the fields of art and design and business, we were able to reinforce and consolidate learning by returning to key skills throughout the course to ensure student mastery of key competences. Learning to navigate the vast number of BTEC units and learning outcomes so as to maximise credits AND student learning is a serious challenge for CP coordinators who are also coordinating the BTEC qualifications.

Making knowledge relevant

The CP allows students the possibility to specialise and it provides them with clear and achievable targets, but to maintain student motivation on a day-to-day basis we need to take the time to make the learning explicitly relevant to the student and the career area. The Personal and Professional Skills (PPS) component at the core of the CP (Language Development; Service Learning; Reflective Project; PPS), teaches practical office skills such as touch-typing and computer literacy, independent research skills, entrepreneurship, business ethics, international mindedness, supplementary language acquisition, and presentation skills. It is here that we frequently hosted guests from industry. For the most part the students felt it was exciting to interact with professionals, but many of our partners sent different employees every time. The most successful connection with industry was the head of professional education at PwC in Geneva, who came back frequently enough to get to know the students and gain their trust. He was even able to review their assignments and give them feedback. I soon learnt that the partnerships, which were most important were not those with companies but with those individuals who were able to commit to long term involvement in the students' learning.

We used the PPS course as a time to brainstorm and create Service Learning projects that were also linked to the students' career-related studies and would allow them to develop skills and their portfolios while serving the community. They organised a careers evening at the school, inviting over a dozen professionals to speak to students and coach them regarding important career decisions. The evening involved two keynote speakers, filmed by our CP students taking the DP Film course, with a catered meal organised largely by students interested in hospitality, and the logistics and marketing of the evening were run by our business students.

The triumph of the CP: graduate successes

Eighteen students started the CP in September 2013. Two left after Year 12, one with a high school diploma and the other because her parents were relocated. The other 16 all achieved the CP and went on to university. The real success story lies in the transformation of CP students from passive, largely apathetic students with weak academic profiles, to learners who became deeply and actively involved in at least one facet of the school community. For some, the DP Film course triggered their transformation; for others the trigger was the Reflective Project, or BTEC's modular approach to assessment, which meant that they could finally get good grades after years of stacking failing grades on top of other failing grades. Students who had given up on academic work ended the programme putting in long days in the library and turning up of their own accord for extra support. Of course, the credit also goes to the teachers, but these same teachers would have felt hamstrung had it not been for the flexibility of the CP.

Some CP students chose the programme because they loved art and design or business. These students were always going to succeed. Most CP students, however, at least in our first cohort, chose the CP because they disliked certain subjects or because they had never enjoyed 'normal school' and they wanted to try an option that was promising to be different. Many of these students tested in the bottom quartile of the CEM ALIS (Centre for Evaluation and

Monitoring Advanced Level Information System) test run by the University of Durham, which is an accurate benchmark test for predicting DP success. Most students knew by the end of Year 11 that there was no way they could study the DP successfully and that the CP was their only viable option to have a last shot at a successful post-16 education.

I have already stated that by the end of Year 13, these students were transformed and their CEM ALIS value-added scores were impressive. It is equally impressive that all of them went to university and they are happily succeeding in their university studies. Table 1 shows the students and the universities that offered them places. The institutions in bold font are the universities and courses they are currently attending. After the table I have included a handful of quotations from students and parents about the CP.

Student	Universities offering places
1	University College Birmingham (Business), University of Northampton (Business), Norwich City College (Business), **IHTTI Neuchâtel (Hotel Management)**
2	Bath Spa University (Business), University College Birmingham (Business), University of Kent (Business) and **University of Plymouth (Business)**
3	**Buckinghamshire New University (Photography)** and Exeter College (Photography)
4	University College Birmingham (Hospitality), Bournemouth and Poole College (Tourism), University of Gloucestershire (Tourism), University of Northampton (Tourism), York St John University (Tourism), **Les Roches (Hotel Management)**, Glion Institute (Hospitality)
5	**University College Birmingham (Business)**, University of Northampton (Business), St Helen's College (Business)
6	**Glion Institute of Higher Education (Hospitality)**, Les Roches (Hospitality), Webster University Geneva (Business)
7	Arts University Bournemouth (Graphic Design), University of Creative Arts (Graphic Design), Leeds College of Art (Graphic Design), **Plymouth College of Art (Graphic Design)**
8	University College Birmingham (Culinary Arts), Bournemouth and Poole College (Culinary Arts), **City College Brighton (Culinary Arts)**
9	London Metropolitan (Interior Design), University of the Arts London (Foundation Year), **Savannah College of Art and Design (Fine Art)**
10	**Webster University Geneva (Liberal Arts)**
11	**University of the Sunshine Coast Queensland (Business)**
12	**Met Film School London (Film)**
13	**University of Sussex (International Business Management)**, Strathclyde University (Business), University of Essex (Business)
14	**Ecole Condé Lyon (Fine Art)**
15	**University of Namibia (Law)**, Fontys University Eindhoven (Business)
16	**Webster University Geneva (Liberal Arts)**

Table 1: Universities offering places to CP students at Ecolint

Feedback on the CP at Ecolint

The comments below reflect the typical reactions that I have received by email from parents and students. They were written after the first year of university and one year after graduation.

From the parents of J:

"The IBCP programme was just fantastic for J. It prepared him really well and gave him a solid grounding for his studies in hospitality. He went into the course with an advantage over other kids, and this was made very clear to us on a recent visit to Glion. During that visit we got talking to one of the teachers there who was so impressed when we told him about J's programme and what he did (specifically in terms of the reflective project he did on ecotourism, and all of the community service). He told J that he needed to emphasise these things when he would be having interviews for his internships (which he is starting to have now), as not many of the other students had shown that amount of initiative and interest in their work."

From student H:

"I'm studying Food and Culinary art course in City College Brighton, UK. I've almost done my first year in college and I will be going back to Malaysia for internship starting April until June. I'm enjoying my course because it has various subjects such as the nutrition and food environment (e.g food waste, water waste, sustainability) as well as practical cooking skills.

Currently, I'm doing a report for business plan. It is same as what I did with you and Mr.T in the past. Most of my assessment that I done was academic writing. In addition, I'm also applying using research methods and am creating a portfolio similar that I done in art class before. It (CP) is very helpful for me to adapt to this course. I'm also still joining English support class to improve my writing and speaking."

From student K:

"It is a challenging program because, as a student, there are always improvements to be made, but I am loving my time here so far as I am constantly learning new things. This program has us working through courses every day of the week with an average of six hours of practical and two and a half hours of class a day. Even though this is not like other "typical" universities as it is very hands on and does not allow a lot of time off for their students, I would highly recommend it to anyone interested in this industry. The CP prepared me for the current challenges I have to face today by giving me insight on what I want to do in the future. It also helped me with improving my time management skills and taught me to set goals for myself."

From student L's parents:

"At this point they are doing things that he did in his HL Film course. He is only one of two people who has ever held a real camera and shot a film. He is doing a lot of outside work – last week he worked on a music video, the week before he helped a graduate student, a few months before an older student (he acted in the film). It seems to us almost every weekend he's either shooting, acting or editing for someone else. I think L was pleased to find that he is more than prepared. He is one of the youngest in his class. There is more writing than he anticipated, but he's been writing and writing well! Surprise!"

One of the early struggles with the CP was university recognition and getting parents to believe in the programme. University recognition is not such an issue anymore, not because the CP is widely known, but because, if you are teaching DP courses and BTEC level 3 units, those qualifications are widely recognised in and of themselves. It would be wonderful to see more recognition for all the work that goes into the core of the CP, but if the core is focused on developing student portfolios and career-related experience these can be a huge benefit when it comes to personal statements, university essays or interviews.

As for parents, word of mouth is starting to help, and the CP's ability to respond to the individual needs of a student with the flexibility the DP simply does not have is bound to add to its appeal. Students who are now in university all say how helpful the career-related focus was and feel that it has given them a head start on many of their peers. Now, as Ecolint's second CP cohort graduates, we feel more fortunate than ever to be able to offer the IB Career-related Programme to our students.

References

Charter of the Foundation of the International School of Geneva (2011): International School of Geneva website. Available at: www.ecolint.ch

Chapter 13

Berlin Brandenburg International School: the Career-related Programme as a commitment to inclusive education

Peter Kotrc and Julia Peters

Beginnings

Monday morning around 8.45 and first-year IB Career-related Programme (CP) student, Bart is busy piecing together the humerus and scapula, readily assisted by one classmate, whilst another names the bones with the help of a website. Their teacher looks on, stepping in with occasional advice and questions, as skeleton 'Sam' gradually takes shape. After this practical introduction to a unit on *Principles of Anatomy and Physiognomy in Sport* the students move on to their next class, IB Diploma Programme (DP) Business Management, in which they are learning about different types of business organisations. After lunch there is a talk from a visiting dermatologist as part of a cross-curricular project on tattoos. Having investigated the topic from both scientific and cultural perspectives, the students are now planning to run a henna tattooing stall at the school's 25th anniversary celebration. For some of them, this will be their first Service Learning activity in the two-year CP.

At the same time Bart's twin brother Klaas is busy with his DP, on this day comprising Standard Level Biology followed by Higher Level Economics and Theory of Knowledge. Yet only a few years previously, the siblings would have been obliged to stick it out in the same programme – regardless of career aspirations, aptitudes and learning styles.

Since its founding in 1990, immediately after German reunification, Berlin Brandenburg International School (BBIS) had been graduating a steadily increasing number of DP students, starting with the first tiny cohort of three candidates in 1997. Ten years later the school could already look back on an intense phase of growth including the purchase and redevelopment of a substantial campus in the leafy outskirts of Berlin. Listed buildings had been fully refurbished as well as adding a state-of-the-art gym, sports field and boarding school facilities. It was time to begin rethinking the school's educational programme for post-16 year olds.

Though fully committed to the IB continuum of international education – IB Primary Years Programme (PYP) and IB Middle Years Programme (MYP) authorisation followed close on the heels of the DP – a few years into the new millennium it was becoming clear that an alternative to the DP was needed for some students. By this time between 30 and 40 students were taking the rigorous, academically focused, pre-university DP each year, roughly 10% of whom were experiencing significant difficulties or even failing to complete the full diploma.

As BBIS is an inclusive school, teachers and administrators alike were motivated to ensure that all students received the opportunity to "fulfil their unique potential" (BBIS Mission and Philosophy). Previously there had been attempts to modify the DP and subject syllabi in order to accommodate some of the learners. This strategy had proved unsatisfactory for various reasons: students were left with a timetable and programme that lacked any coherence, and missed the experience of an interconnected, holistic programme; the general style and pace of learning proved too challenging, despite modifications; and in trying to fulfil the demanding requirements of the DP, students were obliged to take subjects with which they knew they would struggle.

Thus 2009 ushered in the school's own new high school diploma track. After beginning with only a handful of five students – reminiscent of the early days as a DP school – the group grew quickly as did the resolve to switch to the IB's latest programme, then called the IB Career-related Certificate, the IBCC. Some of the school's already successfully trialled high school diploma components such as internships and a focus on business were retained within the IBCC, now the CP, framework which clearly promised to provide a more viable international educational programme based on the kinds of values and learning the IB stands for. Though still at pilot stage, the high school principal believed in the fledgling CP. The parents' trust in the quality of IB programmes was another reason to seek authorisation. Nevertheless, the decision to offer the CP from 2011 required a leap of faith.

Five Pillars

What were the biggest tasks and challenges at the start of our CP journey? Based on our experience at BBIS we can say that the successful implementation of the CP rests on five pillars: budget and resources; information and promotion; the right choices; CP champions; and a good portion of grit. Let us explain these in turn.

Budget and resources

Staff, facilities, educational resources, professional development. Though BBIS was already a fully functioning school in 2011, money and resources had to be allocated to the new programme. For example, the CP core components (Personal and Professional Skills; Service Learning; Language Development; the Reflective Project) were added to the timetable, a coordinator assigned and teachers undertook required training. Considering the small number of students anticipated, and actually enrolled, at the start, this meant a courageous long-term commitment to the programme from the school leadership and governing board.

Information and promotion

'What is the CP? 'How is it different from the DP?' 'What further educational pathways are open to CP graduates?' These were just some of the many questions that students and parents asked from the outset. Up to this day, providing information about the programme and promoting its unique benefits have remained key tasks for the CP coordinator. It is important to note that our school's college and careers counsellor is similarly instrumental in informing and supporting CP students and parents. The counsellor also disseminates information about the CP amongst tertiary education providers, and forges links with individual colleges and universities that are well-matched to our programme. Networking with other CP schools, coordinators and careers counsellors is yet another field that has contributed to building an effective programme.

The right choices

The CP provides a flexible framework, an aspect which cannot be emphasised enough. It means that schools across the world have a considerable degree of freedom to create very different versions of the CP. It is interesting to speculate whether a much more varied CP landscape is in the making compared to the recognisable and well-established edifice of the DP.

At BBIS we decided that learning about business should be the centrepiece of our programme design. Hence the DP Business Management course and biannual internships, though not a CP requirement, are key parts of our curriculum. To match this, external accreditation of our programme was initially guaranteed by a local business college. This combination has proved to be a good fit as evidenced by the number of CP graduates who enrol in university business studies courses, plan to join family companies or aspire to become young entrepreneurs. It is no coincidence that DP Business Management has proved to be the most popular DP course choice for CP schools worldwide.

To further enhance the career focus, a couple of years later we added the UK vocational qualifications, BTEC courses; the subjects Sport as well as Travel and Tourism appearing to be the most appropriate new options for our students. This step involved some carefully thinking about the specific makeup of our student population. Thanks to the school's outstanding sports facilities, a strong physical education programme and numerous extra-curricular activities, many of our students excel in sports. We also have a large percentage of multilingual children from families in the diplomatic service or international business who travel extensively and are inter-culturally knowledgeable and experienced. With this in mind, offering further career-related learning for professions in sports and hospitality seemed the right way to go. The CP's flexibility, however, also means that schools are obliged to make many choices – with room for error. The CP architects at our school were faced with questions such as: Will the chosen career focus suit all our students and attract them to the programme? How can we ensure that the DP courses complement the career-related study and CP core? Do other (e.g. national) requirements need to be met and, if so, how will these be integrated? Later in this chapter we will outline some of the ideas we are currently reconsidering with a view to adjusting our CP design, because despite the best intentions we didn't get everything right from the start. To echo the words of the IB Guide to School Authorization: Career-related Programme (2016), implementing the CP truly "is a *journey...*".

CP champions

We have had a dedicated teacher who tirelessly searched for ways to make her science course accessible to CP students and initiated a market garden as one solution. We have had a mother who enthusiastically told other parents about her son's successes in the CP. We have had a student who stunned the school community by organising a truck to transport aid donations all the way to Kurdistan, and another who secured a place at one of the most renowned design colleges in the US. Building up a successful CP is a team effort, and administrators and coordinators are well advised to look out for those CP advocates and ambassadors who wholly subscribe to the programme and bring out its best. Bear in mind, though, that special projects, noteworthy achievements and shining examples need publicity. Newsletters and brochures, websites and social media, special awards and assemblies are just some of the tools we have used to celebrate the champions that every evolving programme needs.

Grit

Just as grit has been identified as a crucial ingredient to success in learning in general, schools poised to introduce the CP will similarly need a good portion of stamina, persistence and resilience – grit! As mentioned, mistakes in programme design might be made; providing the best choice for every CP student may prove impossible; teachers, students and parents can be resistant to change and distrustful of an educational programme that is still in its infancy. We've been faced by all of these challenges at BBIS.

To this day we have to confront negative perceptions of the CP as 'only a fallback option' in case students can't take the DP, which is still generally regarded more highly by our school community. Fortunately success stories have provided a counterbalance. So far we've seen 60 students graduate from the CP, young people who have experienced their final school years as a time of positive personal achievement instead of crushing failure. Though it is yet too early to determine how well the CP has equipped them for their careers in the long term, we can happily report that our graduates have gone on to university studies or professional training in a wide variety of fields, for example embarking on courses in business, hospitality, design, sports, film or the military.

Other perspectives provide valuable insight into the IB's fourth programme, so the following sections will present feedback from BBIS students and teachers. This will be rounded off with thoughts expressed by other international schools in Germany currently considering the programme. As our own unique CP journey continues, some reflection and an outline of future plans will conclude this chapter.

"It was the better choice for me"

Two round-table conversations took place with two different cohorts of students from year one and year two of the CP. The result is a multi-facetted picture of what the programme looks like in practice for the students. At BBIS, CP students make up 10-20% of their year group, usually 12-15 students. This forms a key element in the students' evaluation and perception of the CP; it is a class a size which allows for a strong and positive group identity which is then perceived as doing something special. While their peers in the DP rarely attend all of their courses with the same students due to their individual subject choices, CP students spend most of the day in the same group as we have opted for a separate set CP timetable. This naturally leads to better social cohesion and team spirit. Our CP students experience the interaction with teachers as better compared with what they hear from other students in the DP. Teachers are seen as being "more chilled" with them and treat them as the more mature student group. It helps that classes in the CP are small.

However, it is surprising how the self-awareness of two year groups in the CP differs. One group feels that it is looked down upon by the students in the DP. They already had a similar experience during the decision-making process between the two programmes in Grade 10, when they heard from a few teachers that "unless you work harder, you will have to do the CP", or when their assessment results were interpreted as showing that they were not ready for six academic DP courses. This group interprets their different programme as indicating that they are not on an equal level with the rest of the year group.

The second cohort, one year younger, sees itself in a much more positive light. A number of them had been admitted to both the DP and CP, and had decided that the CP was indeed "the better choice" for them. These students are the opinion leaders in the group, pulling the rest along in the conversations we had. Their level of information about, and insight into the nature, of the CP makes them feel proud of the path they are taking. All agreed that it was not their parents making a decision for them but it was their own, based on how they saw themselves, their strengths and weaknesses.

Both year groups stress the positive effect of internships and field trips on their independence. The hands-on time in companies, being treated in most cases like normal employees, boosts their self-confidence. The real-life exercise of having to apply for an internship, write a CV and be interviewed (as happens in most cases) adds a reflective loop to their learning which they see DP students are not necessarily experiencing.

It cannot be said whether the second, younger and more positive group has developed the view of its status and the CP from a more sensitive introduction of the two programmes by the school as two equally valid but different routes into tertiary education or the working world. One option BBIS is currently considering is to set up mixed CP/DP classes in certain subjects, e.g. DP Business Management, to highlight the equal value of the programmes. The caveat here is that weak CP students might form a weaker subset in DP courses which could have exactly the opposite effect. Also, the CP identity, as long as it is seen as an advantage, might to some extent disappear which would be regrettable. The next years will tell if such an integration does indeed make sense.

From the classroom: teachers' reflections, evaluations and no definite solutions

The livelihood of all new programmes stems from teachers' enthusiasm and their pride in leading an exciting development in their school. In a round-table discussion, BBIS teachers who just had started teaching the CP, and veterans who had already taught the first ever BBIS CP cohort, reflected on their experience and evaluated how successful the route to life after school was for the students so far.

Observations, impressions and judgements differed considerably. The common denominator in their views was that every international school needs a pathway for students who are simply overwhelmed, for various reasons, by the purely academic DP. How to recognise and nurture their individual talents while keeping them integrated in the peer group is seen as one of the big challenges. Having DP and CP students in the same class, where possible, was a desired option, with the caveat of potentially creating separation within the class, thus creating the opposite effect. Being taught together could act against the perceived loss of motivation of CP students who often feel they are not challenged enough. But will the CP then become some form of "DP lite" programme and not take the range of special abilities of CP students – the practical abilities and the often strong social and communication skills – into account? A suggestion was to continue to offer BTEC courses as part of the CP as their continuous assessment obviously suits our students more than studying for a distant final exam. Still, we must not forget that the CP is a career-related programme and not a vocational course, so the rigour of the three DP courses does indeed provide the right balance.

Internal marketing within a mid-size school was also considered essential by the group of CP teachers: too many colleagues still see the CP (which they seem not to know enough about) as the second choice and reportedly use it as a threat when it comes to programme choices for Grade 10 students.

The CP teachers also recognised the importance of project-based learning, but what is the right project format to nurture independence and deeper learning more effectively than teacher-prescribed tasks? Running model businesses, small enterprises or even the school's successful market garden were all seen as desirable options.

A dilemma which probably cannot be resolved became clear in the discussion amongst the teachers: if we give the CP a very special profile so that students stand out, they may well feel isolated. If we keep to the mantra "same but different" – where is their identity? A good step could be to assign a small group of teachers only to teach the CP components and coach CP students in order to create a coherent, special learning experience.

On the threshold: two German international schools consider the CP

In April 2016 a group of colleagues from Bavarian International School, Munich, and the International School of Hamburg visited BBIS to find out more about the CP. Similar questions and concerns emerged during our conversations, alongside similar aims and hopes connected to a possible introduction of the CP. The following section outlines our colleagues' considerations as they stand at the CP threshold. Obviously their perspective on the CP is influenced by the context we work in as international schools in Germany.

James Dalton, Hamburg's DP Coordinator, explained the current situation at his school:

> "There's a significant number – not the majority – of students for whom the DP is not appropriate, and we're forcing them into quite emotionally challenging, stressful situations with academic subjects they're not suited to. I'm left with little option but to try and get them through ... As a result of this I spend quite a lot of time dealing with a lot of psychological issues, with parents and families – that can't be right. So we need an alternative. The CP is probably much more relevant in today's work place, in the future of further education and employment." (Dalton, 2016)

At Bavarian International School, Jennifer Legan saw the school's high school diploma that she coordinates as a "tough sell because it holds no currency in Europe", whereas the CP "seems like a viable option… that would 'buy' the students something after school" (Legan, 2016).

Nevertheless, both schools have reservations about the programme. With a sigh of frustration, Dalton revealed they have been looking at the CP at the International School of Hamburg "for almost an academic year ... without getting much further." So what is holding them back?

Legan believes the school board of Bavarian International School is cautious about the budgetary commitment involved in introducing the CP, adding that there seems to be a sense that all resources should go towards the DP. A clear cost analysis is needed at Hamburg International School, and Dalton also emphasised the importance of appointing a CP coordinator: "The next stage for us, for it to really take off, is for somebody to be put into a position where their primary responsibility is to drive, to build and to plan the programme."

Another obstacle to the introduction of the CP is designing a strong programme and this involves making many crucial choices. Dalton recognised that "we need a plan that's carefully thought out so it doesn't go off with half measures. Otherwise students won't take it seriously." He described how "the IB leaves a lot of things open to make it very flexible for schools – context is king – that's great! But sometimes a bit of prescription might help. Getting going is quite daunting". Introducing a new career-related course – possibly from an unfamiliar system such as the BTEC – especially requires carefully thinking and planning. It appears to be a bit of a chicken-and-egg situation: costs can only be calculated accurately once the CP has been fully designed, but making sure someone has time to draw up a well-designed programme already requires the allocation of funds.

At Bavarian International School plans are sketchy too, but components that could work well within the CP framework have already been identified. Business would be the chosen career focus – as in many CP schools – so the fact that they already offer the DP Business Management course is an advantage. In fact, Legan is sure that her school could make the CP "work very, very well within the framework we have." Internships, though not a required component of the programme, would be "fundamental" to their programme, and the school is already going about establishing business contacts, for example with a multinational hotel chain.

Legan concludes by giving a positive forecast: "I see the CP as the future of the IB", even going so far to predict that it may become more popular than the DP in twenty years time. "Nowadays it's all about college or university-based education but we need to have kids that know how to work and communicate with other people... that's what the CP does." The International School of Hamburg's DP Coordinator also points out the advantages of the CP:

> "Students have to feel empowered through acquiring the kind of skills they'll need for the workplace. In the DP these are often implied ... and I think there's a group of students, particularly those who can't access the academic courses, who would benefit from something more explicitly vocational to help prepare them for future careers."

Nevertheless Legan anticipates an "uphill battle" because the CP will still be perceived as a fallback plan at her school. Similarly, Dalton maintains that the CP needs to become "a genuine alternative to the DP with equal status". He cautions that it will need the "right level of flexibility and the right level of support from teachers. That's going to take money and investment in the first place."

At the time of writing, both schools are still in the process of deciding whether to introduce the CP.

The journey continues

Building up and fully establishing the CP at BBIS continues to be a journey. The current school year has brought further changes to the timetable: all our CP students have begun taking Standard Level Mathematical Studies as a third DP course, and BTEC Art and Design has been introduced as an additional career-related course. Our aim is to increase the academic rigour whilst giving students a better chance to complete satisfactorily the required minimum of two DP courses. Offering a third BTEC option will enable us to attract students who are artistically inclined and see their future in the field of design. Besides these changes, the improvement of our existing curriculum is ongoing, and the latest revisions to the CP from the IB necessitate further adjustments.

Another change, possibly more fundamental, is the planned integration of CP and DP students in shared DP courses, which has already been mentioned in this chapter. Since the launch of the CP in 2011, DP English and business management courses have been taught in separate CP and DP classes, although the syllabus is identical, with additional weekly periods timetabled for CP students. This choice was firstly for practical reasons: given that CP students have to leave school for work placements twice per year, separate groups ensured they would not miss lessons. Secondly, we have found that CP students benefit from extra time spent on DP courses that often prove to be the most challenging courses on their schedule. With each change we make, though, we have to exercise caution. Will adding a third DP course place too much emphasis on academic learning and alienate exactly those students we are trying to cater for? Do we risk losing the unique career orientation of the CP, indeed turning it into a mere 'DP light' programme?

Concerns of a curricular, practical and social nature are intertwined. Separately run DP courses have led to a detrimental degree of segregation between senior students. However, better integrating our CP and DP students' timetables only seems possible by changing the way we run our internships, which have proved to be one of the most effective components of our CP over the years. We clearly need to strike a balance, maintaining the quality of these important learning experiences outside school, whilst striving to enhance the structures in school.

Even after we have tackled this challenge, more adjustments to the curriculum and timetable are likely to lie ahead. Currently our programme is still somewhat reliant on a 'dual award': our CP graduates also receive a high school diploma, the latter being the entrance ticket to some university systems, which do not yet recognise the CP. This means that our timetable has to include additional courses required for a high school diploma that go beyond the requirements of the CP. The result is a wide and varied curriculum, but one that possibly lacks depth and focus on career-related learning.

To date, university recognition of the CP remains key to ensuring the ongoing success of our programme. The list of colleges and universities that accept the CP as an entrance qualification is growing; the UK is an especially positive example in this respect and particularly relevant in our school's European context. Yet in Germany, CP graduates can only apply to private colleges as the educational authorities do not recognise the programme as yet. Thus we continue to run the CP in an unsupportive national context.

As our college and careers counsellor continues the quest to gain CP recognition from individual colleges, the IB lobbies with university systems at a national level. Though this is important work, surely we also need to reinforce and develop other pathways beyond school for CP graduates? If the CP is to be a truly career-related alternative to the DP, serving more practically-minded, hands-on learners, then we should avoid a fixation on university-based, tertiary education. Instead we should also be forming partnerships with industries so that the CP gains currency as an excellent preparation for apprenticeships, other professional training schemes or immediate employment.

Steps in this direction are being taken. In June 2016 the IB announced the launch of a newly designed *CISI Diploma in Finance, Risk and Investment* as an option for the CP career-related study. Designed in collaboration with the UK Chartered Institute of Securities and Investments, this course may serve as a blueprint for future partnerships between the IB, schools and businesses, a model that could propel the CP forward and ensure it thrives in the 21st century. As the IB's UK Recognition and Development Manager, Dr Peter Fidczuk, predicts: "This partnership is just the first of many in the UK, showing the IB's commitment to progressing learning partnerships across diverse sectors."

Another development may help shift us away from a fixation on university education. With a new generation of stand-alone CP schools on the horizon, the IB will be entering a different arena of post-16 educational providers that will in turn open up alternative, career-focused pathways beyond school.

Despite the challenges, ongoing improvements and open questions, without a doubt the CP has been the right addition to BBIS. Our experience has shown that the programme nurtures the values and attitudes that all IB World Schools aspire to, preparing 21st century youngsters to enter the world of work with intercultural understanding, communicative competence, critical thinking and ethical behaviour.

Just as the BBIS twins, Bart and Klaas, end their school day together engaged in various extracurricular activities – basketball, soccer, Duke of Edinburgh Award, Habitat for Humanity – we look towards a future in which the Career-related and Diploma Programmes will prosper side by side and become true equals.

References

Dalton, J. (2016): Personal interview, 14 April.

International Baccalaureate (2016): *Guide to School Authorization: Career-related Programme.* The Hague, Netherlands: International Baccalaureate.

Legan, J. (2016): Personal interview, 14 April.

Chapter 14

Implementing the Career-related Programme at Greenfield Community School, Dubai: a coordinator's tale

Mike Worth

Education is undergoing considerable change as we strive to meet the needs of students in today's changing world. Learning styles, integrating digital technology, resources, research skills ... the development is just vast. I am now in my 32nd year as a teacher and when I think of the difference from my first year until now, it's almost incomprehensible. I often reflect back to my days as a young student when I struggled so much because of the labels 'non-academic' and 'less able'. The fact was that I did not enjoy sitting in classes for long periods writing copious amounts from a board which I had to remember, and then being tested through an examination. I found it hard and it wasn't for me. If I was a student today I would probably be identified as having special educational needs, but the simple fact is that I knew what I was good at and preferred practical tasks, being active and creative, designing and making things and I loved all sports. But give me a text book to learn from and an examination to sit, and it was game over.

Sir Ken Robinson, the renowned educationalist and presenter of many TED talks, consistently questions teaching and learning methods and the relevance of examinations in today's world. The world today is full of people who have not completed a traditional academic, examination-based education; they do not have a degree but are successful. Robinson advocates the need to teach creativity and life skills as compulsory subjects in the same way that English, mathematics and science are 'core' subjects (Robinson, 2010). Research on successful leaders such as Sir Richard Branson, Bill Gates and Steve Jobs, identifies key factors which have helped to make them successful and which are about life skills, rather than whether they achieved a degree (Bel, 2010). I have always felt these skills should be taught and developed in schools and should be seen as equally important. The educational landscape today is changing, as it has to in order to meet the needs of a changing society and the age in which we live. Robinson argues that we are preparing today's students for a future of which we are very unsure. So what do they need to enable them to succeed in a career of their choice in such an uncertain world?

Having taught in the UK, Australia and now Dubai, specialising in vocational education, I was delighted when the International Baccalaureate (IB) began to develop the Career-related Programme (CP). What excited me the most was that I saw a bridge between the academic and the vocational. There has long been debate about the two approaches, with many people viewing vocational courses as less rigorous or challenging than academic courses. The IB has had the foresight to combine both in one programme. The other key characteristic which is so important, and which I will mention many times, is that the CP is a framework which can be designed and developed to meet individual and local needs. There are three parts to the CP: the career-related studies (BTEC for Greenfield Community School); DP courses; and four CP core components – Language Development; Service Learning; Personal and Professional Skills; the Reflective Project. Through these three parts, the programme can be adapted to suit the individual student, school or local/national environment. An academic programme is often made up of separate subjects with prescribed content and an examination at the end; the career-related study element of the CP is career-specific and usually linked to industry standards. The combining of these two approaches is a major factor in the appeal of the CP.

The context

I have been the CP coordinator at Greenfield Community School, Dubai, since it was a pilot CP school in 2011. Greenfield is an international private school, opened in 2007, and part of a group of schools managed by a company called Taaleem which currently operates 11 schools in the United Arab Emirates. In 2011 Greenfield offered the IB Primary Years Programme (PYP), IB Middle Years Programme (MYP), and the IB Diploma Programme (DP). It was clear that offering only the DP for the final two years of schooling was not meeting the needs of all our students and that the opportunity to offer the CP would add so much more. We had seen our student numbers grow as we developed from the PYP into MYP, and Greenfield was soon only one of a handful of IB World Schools (schools authorised by the IB to teach one or more of its programmes) offering all four IB programmes. We have a healthy enrolment of 1,500 students with 86 different nationalities, illustrating the international nature of Dubai.

As a growing city and country, the change in Dubai over the past 30-40 years has been remarkable, to the point where it is now a global centre for trade, industry, travel and tourism. The rate of change has been phenomenal and this has resulted in a rapidly expanding population now reaching 8.5 million, the majority of whom are expatriates who have come to Dubai for work and opportunity. With such a diverse and international population the educational landscape has needed to accommodate the different nationalities and cultures. Dubai has its local schools, dedicated to the Emirati population, but it also has schools offering a range of curricula from the UK, Europe, the US and Canada, Asia and Australasia, as well as the international IB programmes. When I first came to Dubai many students would leave school at the end of Grade 10, at the age of 16, to return to their own countries for the final two years of their education. But this is changing dramatically, with over 80% of students now staying in Dubai with their families and taking advantage of the educational opportunities on offer. The CP is growing in popularity across schools in Dubai as it offers not only a highly regarded international curriculum, but also a programme that meets the needs of all learners. This is a significant development and I relish the anticipated growth of this programme over the coming years.

Getting started

My initial contact with the CP came in 2011 when Greenfield became a pilot CP school. It was already a well-established IB World School offering a wide range of DP courses. We began our CP venture with a small group of enthusiastic students. In the first year the entry requirements for the CP were not prohibitive; we knew we had to start somewhere with as many students as we could.

The first weeks of implementing the CP were challenging and, as with anything new, judgements were made quickly. Many DP students were highly critical of the new programme and its students. Comments such as 'it's so easy', and 'you're not good enough for the DP' were heard. This was disappointing as we were rightly proud of being one of the first schools to be given the opportunity to pilot the CP. But the reality soon hit home: as soon as you offer two options, one will be seen as better than the other. Another problem was what parents thought of the new programme. In one of the first parent information sessions I was immediately asked: 'How does this get my son into university?' That was a hard one as the CP, in the early days, was not seen as a university entry programme. Other questions were: 'Is it accepted in other countries?' and 'Does it have equivalency?' These were questions that just could not be answered satisfactorily in the early days of the programme. I was also interested to observe some negativity from parents when the word 'vocational' was mentioned. Having come through a vocational route myself as a student, and seeing how good it could be, I was disappointed to see this attitude. I had been teaching in Australia for 16 years where vocational education was seen as a good option for many students; not every student could go to university and, arguably, not every student should go to university. But the majority of Greenfield parents, in our first year of the CP, had a degree of negativity about this type of career-related education. They only had one idea of future education for their child, and that was university.

When I review my role as CP coordinator at Greenfield I often smile as I think of how many changes it has gone through. I have to be a 'Jack of all trades', and flexible in so many situations so that the title of coordinator is not quite accurate. At the start, due to the small numbers of students opting for the CP, I was the only person teaching the programme, which can't have been easy for the students, seeing me every day, teaching both the CP core components and BTEC subjects (see below). In hindsight, it would have been better to have a small team with which to collaborate and I would advise any new school starting the CP that having a team really does help.

What follows is a description of how Greenfield Community School has implemented the three parts of the CP and adapted them to suit the students and the school context.

(a) The career-related study: BTEC

The introduction of the BTEC (Business and Technical Education Council) courses as our career-related studies at Greenfield was challenging but exciting. BTEC is a UK-based organisation providing specialist, work-related qualifications for school leavers and those who want to go into higher education. BTEC courses are offered in over 140 countries and are aimed specifically at the 16-19 age group. BTEC currently offers over 40 subjects, written and developed with the support of industry bodies. It therefore has credibility and recognition and is a perfect fit for the CP as the career-related study component. Successful completion of the career-related study for the CP is directed by the awarding body (BTEC) not the IB. The students were concerned about where this new qualification could take them. Would it be accepted by colleges, universities or employers? This concern was also shared by parents and many staff but, thankfully, we only had to wait for our first cohort to graduate to provide reassurance as all students managed to gain places at international universities (UK, US, Canada, Australia, Dubai) or universities located in their home countries. The CP was so new that many of the universities I contacted had not heard of it, but when I mentioned BTEC courses, they were familiar with them; it became clear that they are highly regarded by both universities and employers. This was very reassuring. Having been a BTEC student myself, studying engineering and product design, and then a teacher of BTEC courses, I was confident that this was the right qualification for us to offer as our career-related study within the CP, but it was an unknown qualification amongst the Greenfield parent community so I knew that I had a lot of work to do with parents and students. The type and structure of the career-related study we offered was a critical element in the development of our Greenfield CP. It was decided that we would offer the full 12-unit BTEC course, regarded as university entry level, to give our students the necessary entry-level qualification should they decide to apply to university. For all the reasons given above, we had to give them that option.

The addition of an external qualification to the CP was an inspired idea by the IB when the format of the programme was first conceived. There are a number of excellent vocational qualifications available for schools around the world. Having taught in the UK where the BTEC is well established and highly regarded, and then moving to Australia where the TAFE (Technical and Further Education) qualification is also highly regarded and monitored by professional organisations, I was aware of at least two possible courses we could offer. In the past the vocational courses have tended to be very specialised and linked to trades but in today's changing world there is a need for students to develop a broad range of transferable skills for which the newer qualifications provide. The BTEC courses also have credibility because all the subjects are created by industry bodies which is advantageous when a student wishes to find employment in a chosen industry. With the CP being so new as a qualification it was important to have a qualification which already had credibility. This is the beauty of the CP: schools can add their own local vocational or career-related study to the CP framework.

The issue we had in our initial planning was quite clear. By offering a BTEC qualification, which subjects would we offer? Vocational courses are usually specific to a skill or profession; there really isn't a broad-based, career-related course that could be used. So in initial discussions with students, the decision was taken to offer the BTEC Level 3 business as our first offering as a career-related study. The first few years of the CP have been successful for our students as business is a more broad-based subject than most, and does offer valuable, transferable skills. Units where students study the business environment, resources, communication, product promotion, retail, human resources management, starting a small business, business ethics and managing a business event are excellent and sufficiently broad that they give students exposure to the working environment.

Timetabling issues, staff and budget constraints make it difficult to offer a wide range of BTEC courses, but offering only one career-related study path severely limits the options of the students. So from a successful start with the CP becoming established at Greenfield and, more importantly, gaining some much needed credibility, we needed to offer more BTEC courses than just business. In surveying the grade 9 and 10 students there was a request for sport, hospitality, and art and design as possibilities. The BTEC art and design course is excellent because it can be offered as a specialist art subject or it can incorporate many optional units from the creative spectrum. The five mandatory units help to develop a range of creative art and design skills; we decided to offer seven units from art and design: 3D design; graphic design; interior design; fashion and textiles; media; photography; IT. The students choosing a BTEC Level 3 National Diploma as their career-related study have access to a programme which offers a breadth of creative work all culminating in the building of an art portfolio which is needed for entry to art college, university or an arts foundation course. From offering only one BTEC course with a specialism in business, to now offering 11 courses is a huge development and one which has helped us to grow the student numbers. We would like to offer other BTEC subjects but we must make sure they are sustainable over a number of years.

One of the other positives in offering a BTEC Level 3 course is that it has credibility in its assessment process. The rules and regulations are very rigorous and must be adhered to if a school is to keep its licence to offer such courses. All student work is internally assessed by the teacher, and further assessed by an internal verifier based within the school. The student work and assessment decisions are then externally verified by a visit from an International Standards Verifier who visits the school twice a year. The reports they produce are extensive and very important, and the feedback is used to plan and improve the BTEC courses.

(b) DP courses

The initial requirement from the IB was that a minimum of two DP courses must be studied at Standard Level. The incorporation of the DP courses is a major part of the CP and offers students the opportunity to develop academic skills and knowledge in subjects that will support their career pathway. With timetabling being a critical factor as the CP developed, initially we kept the DP courses at two, increasing BTEC lessons to cover the 12 units required – the university entry level needed. Extra lessons were added for the Personal and Professional Skills and Language Development components of the CP core, plus one lesson per week for Service Learning as it was important to have this structured time for preparation and planning of events and projects. We currently offer a five-lesson day of 80 minutes per lesson at Greenfield, which allows for all these CP components to be compliant.

In our second year of the CP at Greenfield we had a situation which brought home the potential fragility of the structure of the CP. We had a student who met the requirements for the DP but chose to study the CP with a focus on business. Her intention was to study for a degree and then join the family business. At the end of her CP, her BTEC coursework was outstanding and she gained distinctions in all 12 units. In her CP Reflective Project she achieved a B grade and also a 6 (out of 7) in her language acquisition, English Standard Level class. But in DP maths she achieved only a grade 2 which meant she was not awarded the CP. This was a blow for the student, but, thankfully, she was able to gain a place at her chosen university in the UK by having met the entry requirements through her BTEC Business course. She is now studying for a degree in business in the UK, but it was worrying that one low grade could lead to a student not graduating from the CP. As a result of this situation, it was decided that we would add an additional DP course to the CP at Greenfield, making three DP courses compulsory for all our students, thus providing more options for students to complete successfully the CP. The third course was taken from DP group 2 language acquisition courses, which also meets the requirements of the Language Development (LD) component of the CP core.

(c) The CP core

Language Development

The IB has always promoted the need for students to develop additional languages as well as their own mother tongue; a philosophy strongly supported by Greenfield. But in the initial planning of the pilot CP, getting to grips with the requirements and outcomes of the Language Development component was challenging. If students were learning a language for the first time, how would they become fluent in just two years? Did they need to become fluent? How would they be assessed and how would this be integrated into the rest of the CP core? The CP guides state that the language studied should not be in the mother tongue or strongest language. But in considering the language levels and abilities of many Greenfield students it was clear that some students needed additional support in English to enable them to be successful in their DP courses, which can be written only in English, French or Spanish, as well as the BTEC units which are written in English.

Consequently, in planning the CP, added additional English lessons were added for those students who were identified as in need of them, with the other students studying an additional language. I have heard of many schools offering one language which all students study. Over the past few years my view of the LD component has changed considerably and I view it as a very positive addition to the CP core. As I have previously stated, we offer three DP courses with one being from the DP group 2, language acquisition. Students are able to study a language from the beginning or to further develop an existing language. They are able to use this language for the required LD portfolio and provide key evidence of the development of this additional language. But in trying to develop a more integrated LD programme, a real need for the students to study Arabic was identified – Arabic being local language – especially if they intended to stay and study or work in the United Arab Emirates. So in our additional LD lessons the CP students study Arabic with a focus on learning some basic language and understanding customs and history. As part of our Service Learning programme, the CP students visit Tanzania to support local projects (see Service Learning below), so an additional part of our LD programme is for these students to learn basic Swahili, and gain understanding of the culture, people, customs and history. The LD component has developed well over recent years and a marked improvement in students' confidence and language skills is evident.

The Reflective Project

For many Greenfield students, the Reflective Project has proved to be an extremely challenging part of the CP. Not used to researching an ethical issue of such depth, or writing 3,000 words, this project has tended to be put on the back burner for many students. From the early planning I realised I needed to teach this part of the programme rather than treat it like the extended essay of the DP, where the work is done independently with only periodic meetings with supervisors. Timetabling a lesson each week with a focus on developing a key ethical question and progressing through to a completed quality project has worked; the students feel supported and I am able to guide each one through their individual project. The results over the past few years have not been the best as many have struggled with this work, but the students see the benefit of successfully completing it in terms of skill development for university admissions.

Personal and Professional Skills

New in 2016, the Personal and Professional Skills (PPS) course has taken the career-related focus to a new level. The introduction of the five themes: personal development; intercultural understanding; effective communication; thinking processes; applied ethics, is a considerable development and challenging for the students. At Greenfield we have taken a project-based approach with PPS, with clear deadlines, structured teaching and learning time, and student self-study and reflection. My experience of CP students is that they need structure and guidance and do not always possess self-motivation and study techniques. They respond better to practical tasks which have clear deadlines and achievable goals; time management is a also key factor, as are organisational skills. For a school offering the CP, the PPS should be integrated with other CP components. Linking PPS to the work placement (see below), Service Learning and the career-related study will provide a rich, integrated programme that will benefit the students enormously.

A class project such as creating a school cookbook can cover many aspects of the PPS course. It enables the students to work in groups, meet the needs of a client, work to a deadline and create a quality product or outcome. Watching students work on the cookbook project, it was a delight to see how well they collaborated and communicated. Certainly they argued a lot, but in the end they were of one mind in achieving their goal, which was to produce a product that could be sold, with the proceeds being donated to their chosen charity. Achieving this goal gave each student a huge sense of pride and confidence. There were no examinations, nor the stress of having to remember facts, figures, dates or formulae, but there was real evidence of commitment, motivation and team work. The new PPS course delivers a wonderful combination of the career-related and academic skills needed by today's students.

Service Learning

I have been greatly encouraged by how the CP Service Learning (SL) component has been developed by the IB and how it is become such a significant and beneficial part of the programme. Gone are the days when students take part in a sponsored walk, raise some money for a charity and call it service. SL is a great opportunity to develop key skills and also to link with other areas of the CP. From the initial planning for the CP, we have sought to develop an integrated SL programme which links to other CP components, with the intention of identifying and developing key life skills. The addition of a specific timetabled period to help with the planning, preparation, development and reflection of

SL activities has been invaluable. School-based SL activities are really useful for raising the profile of the CP, but the SL programme really comes alive when it is linked with local, national or international projects.

For Greenfield, as an international school, we needed an international dimension for our SL programme. Local activities are the focus of our involvement and the benefits have been enormous. But three years ago I linked with the International School of Moshi (ISM), an IB World School in Tanzania, which has developed a fantastic programme called 'Go Kili', hosting international schools to spend a week with them to work in their local community on a variety of projects. In the time we have been working with them we have helped local people to build classrooms at a local school. From laying a concrete base to painting the inside and out, it has been a great experience for our students. Meeting and working with the local people from the village, visiting a local orphanage and planting over 200 trees in a village on the slopes of Mount Kilimanjaro have been some of the highlights.

Work placement at Greenfield – an addition to the CP core

The idea of a work placement for students, where they spend a week with a company experiencing the working environment, is not new. Although the CP does not require this as part of the programme, it was the first thing that was added and it is now compulsory at Greenfield. From our first year as a CP pilot school, students have completed three one-week work placement blocks – two in the first year of the CP and the final one in the second year. It is structured in this way to give the students exposure to two different work environments in year one, which can then be further developed in year two to align with their chosen career pathway.

Students select and plan their own placement venue, a key part of the learning process. There is little benefit if the teacher arranges everything, but in PPS they are guided through the whole process: creating their CV, researching the company, contacting the intended company, writing the application, making appointments and preparing for the working environment. There is also the official and legal documentation required by schools when students are 'off campus'. In Dubai, these are not as rigorous as those in the UK or Australia, but nevertheless, they need to be met. I also make a point of going to the company or work environment myself, as a courtesy visit, but mainly to carry out a site inspection and to confirm the requirements and expectations for the placement. Like many teachers who have been involved in a work placement programme, I have experienced ones where students only photocopy or make the coffee. To get around this, some students have 'work shadowed' which has less impact on the company employees. Once the placement has started, I visit each student to monitor their activity at least once, and keep in contact with the student's supervisor in case of problems. Students are also required to complete a daily log, plus a case study which explores the company structure, development, history, sales, etc. This also links with their BTEC Business course for a mandatory unit which explores the business environment. Another great opportunity for integration across the CP.

The success of the work placement programme cannot be overestimated and every student has gained so much from the experience. I believe that a programme such as the CP must have a component of work placement for each student to experience the working environment. Even in areas where activities are restricted, the students can benefit so much just by being exposed to the world of work. I have encountered many companies who have not wished to take students, which is disappointing, so we have developed links with local charities who are always willing to take our students, and students who work for charity organisations often get a broader experience. Two such organisations we have been involved with are the K9 dog sanctuary and Feline Friends cat rescue centre in Dubai. Run by volunteers and through donations, the work they do has given many students a truly valuable experience, enabling them to see how such an organisation operates. Students are more likely to be asked to carry out a wider range of tasks in these environments, and whilst such a placement may not be aligned to a career pathway, the skills the students are exposed to are invaluable and give them so much confidence. For many students this experience cements their chosen career pathway or helps them realise that a certain career path is not for them. For some of our students, the work placement has led to offers of additional internships, summer work placements and even financial support for university study, with the intention of employment after graduation.

Developing an integrated CP

I have already mentioned that a major strength of the CP is that it is a framework rather than a fully prescribed programme. By choosing the BTEC qualification as our career-related study, we had the opportunity to create a programme which was integrated and which would enable all students to develop transferable skills. Academic subjects are often taught in isolation and the knowledge and skills developed within these subjects may not always transfer to other subjects. DP teachers in many schools have limited knowledge of what happens in other subjects, what content is being taught or where opportunities exist for integration. The CP has given us a perfect opportunity to create a project-based, integrated programme where key skills are identified, taught, and then put into practice. For example, in the Level 3 BTEC Business course, there is an optional unit called 'Managing a Business Event'. In this unit students develop knowledge of what a business event is, the role of an event organiser, skills needed, planning and preparation, safety and legal factors. It is a highly challenging and comprehensive unit. So why teach this in isolation?

The CP provides a valuable opportunity to link this project across several of its components, particularly PPS and SL, resulting in the development of a number of other projects such as designing and creating a product which could be sold with profits and linked to a local charity. Our first project was a cookbook which contained recipes to reflect the 86 different nationalities and cultural diversity we have in our school. The CP students have also taken on projects such as the school year book and linking with the school's drama department to manage the promotion of the annual school play, producing tickets, posters, programmes and web pages. These are projects which give students the opportunity to be involved in 'real-life' business events.

Over the past five years, the CP students have worked with the European Golf Tour to assist with the two prestigious golfing events which are held annually in Dubai: the Omega Dubai Ladies Masters Tournament and the Omega Dubai Desert Classic Tournament for the men. Our CP students are involved in these events as course marshals, which involves managing the public at key points on the course, such as tee boxes, on-course crossing points, hospitality areas and the main grandstands. The CP students develop skills in planning, organisation, customer service, teamwork and health and safety, amongst others. They also develop leadership skills, taking on the responsibility for small teams as they perform the duties required across the four days of each tournament. Our CP students are also involved in annual events held in Dubai such as the Dubai Marathon and triathlons where they are responsible for managing facilities such as a drinks station on the course. Supporting local events which involve world class athletes has been such a thrill for our students, even if they have to be on course setting up at 5am!

Each of these projects offers CP students opportunities to integrate knowledge and understanding and develop life skills. These are not made-up or role-play activities, they are real life events. The students realise the responsibility required in being involved with such events, and the sense of pride they feel with a job well done cannot be measured. In planning for the CP, it is important to make activities project-based, integrated with other components of the programme and real.

Examples of CP student pathways at Greenfield

In Greenfield we have had 35 students graduate from the CP and we currently have 42 students studying the programme. I have commented that one of the strengths of the CP is that it is a framework and not a prescribed programme of academic study. To illustrate this strength I will describe the experience of one Greenfield student who graduated in 2014. He had always wanted to focus on business with the intention of studying a business degree in the UK. He was accepted onto the DP but chose the CP because he wanted to specialise in business studies. His career-related study was BTEC Level 3 National Diploma course in Business with 12 units. He chose as his DP courses English Higher

Level and Design Technology Standard Level. His CP Reflective Project also focused on business ethics which fitted in well with his career path of business. He achieved outstanding results in all components of the CP and is now studying for a business degree at Greenwich University, London.

Another CP student, who graduated in 2016, had always wanted to start up her own catering business and had a passion for high quality cakes and decoration. In creating her CP programme, her career-related study was a diploma in catering which she studied at a specialist catering college in Dubai. Her DP courses were Business and Management Standard Level and Visual Arts Higher Level. This student was identified as needing learning support in Grade 8, having moved to Dubai from India. Over the years she received considerable learning support from the school, but this did not deter her from her goals. Witnessing her personal growth during this time was humbling. For this student, the partnership with the local catering college was a key factor as the school could not offer such a high level course in catering nor did it have the facilities. With the support of the IB, which approved the career-related study, she embarked on and completed the diploma in catering with distinction. She has now returned to her home country where she has set up a specialist cake business, working initially from home. She hopes to open her own store soon.

Our students were able to benefit from having a qualification that would meet their individual needs and chosen pathways. As I write this, 31 of our CP graduates are studying at universities around the world, two have taken up employment, one has started her own business and one is doing national service in his own country. I think these outcomes are something to celebrate. This programme truly meets the individual needs of the students and it is able to do this because it is a flexible, adaptable framework: it is not a 'one size fits all' academic programme. It is flexible enough to meet individual needs but can also be set up for a whole cohort. This flexibility can make delivery challenging for teachers and the CP coordinator, but the rewards are considerable. The IB should be acknowledged for the work they have done in developing this innovative programme. The ability to use a framework to create an international programme with a range of career-related studies and links to local specialist colleges is inspiring.

University admissions

With the DP having a rich history as a well-established pathway to universities, it was almost inevitable that the CP would be viewed by many as the poor relation and a lesser qualification. I am still not sure if the CP was ever seen as a university entry qualification, being aimed more at tertiary colleges and entry into employment. But by offering a career-related study such as a BTEC level 3 National Diploma course with 12 units, or even the BTEC Extended Diploma with 18 units, the CP has become a qualification which meets many university entry requirements.

It has not been easy obtaining university recognition for the CP or entry for the students. It has often needed many emails and phone calls to university admissions officers to simply explain what the CP is and how the assessments compare with the DP. I have built up a list of the universities that I know have accepted Greenfield students with a CP qualification and added this to data from other CP coordinators. I have been alarmed at the lack of knowledge and understanding of IB programmes from some university admissions offices, but in order to support our students, we as coordinators and also university counsellors need to continually monitor the situation. Such involvement is also an expectation of an IB school that has piloted a new and innovative programme; CP schools need to work alongside the IB to promote the programme for the sake of the students.

Final reflections

Now in my sixth year of offering the CP at Greenfield Community School I can honestly say it is a fantastic programme. I feel the IB should be commended for creating an innovative, international curriculum framework which is flexible enough to meet the needs of students who are studying in so many countries. Having taught courses such as A Level in the UK and the High School Certificate in Australia, my view is that many such programmes are simply a collection of subjects which are delivered as such, with little or no integration. The CP combines a range of subjects in an integrated way with assessment strategies which allow the students to achieve their potential. The CP really is a programme for the 21st century learner and beyond.

References

Bel, R. (2010): *Leadership and Innovation: Learning from the Best*. Global Business & Organizational Excellence, 29 (2), 47-60.

Robinson, K. (2010): www.ted.com/talks/ken_robinson_changing_education_paradigms

Chapter 15

The Career-related Programme as a catalyst for change: the experience of Renaissance College, Hong Kong

Stewart Redden

If our current educational model is to change then the catalyst for this could be the IB Career-related Programme (CP). Ken Robinson, amongst others, has pointed out that schools in the 21st century are still based on a model devised to provide educated workers for the industrial revolution of the 19th century (Robinson, 2015). In this chapter I will suggest that the CP is the educational programme that could facilitate this desired paradigm shift because it can provide a specialised, experiential education for high school students in environments where professionals work. The current paradigm provides a standardised education in a removed classroom environment, whereas the emerging paradigm provides a personalised education in an environment that actually is, or resembles, the environment where the skills and knowledge students acquire at school will need to be applied.

When the CP was launched it was seen by many educators as a programme for students who couldn't manage the IB Diploma Programme (DP). However, this was to miss the whole point of the new programme, and in the most condescending fashion. In reality, it was the DP that was not providing for the needs of students who wished to follow specialised career paths that had often become their passion, for example in engineering, architecture, hospitality or business. However, accommodating personalised education can be challenging for CP schools in terms of providing a range of offerings that will meet the diverse needs of their students. In this chapter, therefore, I will explore an approach to implementing the CP that is based on collaboration amongst CP schools, enabling them to offer a range of career-related study options through external providers.

The context for this chapter is Renaissance College, Hong Kong. It is a four-programme IB World School that was first established in 2006 as an independent school within the Hong Kong based English Schools Foundation (ESF). It has a diverse student body with more than 40 nationalities and 20 languages represented on campus; it caters mainly to the local community in the vicinity of Ma On Shan in the New Territories but it has a city campus with around 2,100 students from Year 1 to Year 13. In July, 2013 it became the first school in East Asia to offer the CP.

The nature of the CP: flexibility and integration

The CP is the most recent of the four IB programmes available to schools, and it is growing rapidly. Students study between two and four DP courses at Standard Level or Higher Level, and also complete the CP core components: Personal and Professional Skills, Language Development, Service Learning and the Reflective Project. The third part of the programme is the career-related study which enables a student to take, as part of an IB education, a focused, accredited, career-related study such as a course at a local college or university, a technical course or any other accredited course provided internally within the school or externally. This approach allows students to specialise in an area that they are specifically interested in developing as a professional career. The CP also has a centre to its programme model that is consistent with all the other IB programmes: the IB Learner Profile. In a sense the CP is a hybrid model that enables authorised DP schools to use their existing courses and staffing for the DP courses, which constitute about 50% of the CP or more in some schools, while providing students with well recognised and accredited courses for the purpose of furthering their career-related ambitions.

The core of the CP is unique in many ways. It allows for an innovative approach to learning skills development through Personal and Professional Skills (PPS), whereby the course is designed by the school to meet the needs of its students and can, therefore, incorporate practices such as statistical thinking (Nisbett, 2015), recognition of system I and system II thinking (Kahneman, 2011), and practices in effective communication such as the use of the Losada ratio (Seligman, 2011). Because the PPS course is designed by the school within an IB framework, the school can provide students with up-to-date skills more quickly than a traditionally developed curriculum is able to do.

The Reflective Project is also innovative in making the student's specialised career-related study the focus of the ethical dilemmas which are at the heart of this component. This fits well with the emphasis that many universities are now placing on ethical thinking within their degree programmes. The Language Development component allows full flexibility in how the students develop their language skills, from taking courses at external language schools through to students combining their study of DP language acquisition courses along with an extra topic or theme to meet the requirements of the Language Development component. Service Learning in the CP requires the students to make use of their career-related study to put their specialised skills to good use in the local community, and also for their Service Learning to relate to their Reflective Project. Thus, the CP enables a much more integrated approach to skills and service learning than most schools traditionally take, ensuring that they have explicit links with the students' career-related studies.

Evolving the educational model

It is, of course, quite misleading to think that schools haven't developed or improved at all since the inception of the 19th century model of education that provided workers for the industrial revolution. That said, the 19th century model of education has not gone through the paradigm shift that our 21st century world requires; it has been refined and improved incrementally in terms of effectiveness and efficiency, but not changed fundamentally. The general concept of the traditional model of education is that of a removed learning environment, essentially school classrooms, rather than the offices or studios we find in the workplace. Although in this classroom model we may find innovative ways of arranging desks and creating more adaptable space, the core philosophy remains unchanged in that it is, essentially, an artificial, removed environment.

In the CP education can take place outside the traditional classroom setting on a regular basis and in a stimulating and authentic environment. It is, therefore, an educational programme that has the potential to create a revolution. The career-related study, combined with highly respected DP courses, accepted by universities and employers for their academic rigour, provide for the educational experience to be very effective and not just novel. These two aspects rest on the specially designed core, which encapsulates the IB's philosophy and provides a creative approach to support life-long learning effectively. The CP can therefore provide a preparation for students which can give them a significant head start on students coming from traditional educational environments.

At Renaissance College, the CP has been developed in cooperation with the Savannah College of Art and Design (SCAD) which has a campus in Hong Kong, and it has blurred the line between high school and university for our CP students. SCAD is a US-based, private, non-profit, accredited institution of higher education that prepares students for professional careers. When the students travel to the SCAD campus in the afternoons they access facilities that are far beyond what a high school can provide, and they have access to experienced lecturers who are active practitioners in their chosen fields. This environment enables our students to develop a more professional and comprehensive body of work during high school than would be possible if the same students were taking the DP. The afternoons spent at SCAD also provide a wealth of experience that is very attractive to art colleges around the world and, additionally, the students are completing foundation courses which provide university credit for continued study at SCAD or elsewhere. in the first cohort of CP students at Renaissance College, one of the students was admitted to the California Institute of the Arts (CalArts), which continually vies for position as the top art college in the US. I believe that a major factor in this student being selected was because the CP enabled her to develop more fully as an artist than she would have done in a purely academic programme.

I would argue that the art and design students that study the CP, rather than taking visual arts or design technology within the DP, are better equipped for tomorrow's rapidly changing world because they become more effective practitioners within their chosen career pathway more rapidly. I noticed at Renaissance College, before it adopted the CP, and in previous schools in which I have worked, that studying the DP often got in the way of students wanting to go to art and design colleges, as they had to be successful not only in all the components of the DP, but at the same time develop a comprehensive body of quality work for their portfolio, and to develop themselves as artists to pass the required interviews and admissions procedures. Developing specialist knowledge takes a long time, with a figure of 10,000 hours being reported to develop the intuitive skills of a true professional (Kahneman, 2011). Therefore, to give students the best chance to maximise their potential for the subject area that they have pursued with passion, and are fixed upon for their career, the CP is an option that will enable them to reach a professional level more quickly.

The DP courses and the CP core provide robust and innovative learning, while the niche interest of the student is met by the career-related study providers with specialised knowledge and expertise, such as SCAD. The CP structure allows for a full range of approaches to the career-related study, from students taking university and college courses to local technical college courses. In some college-based vocational programmes, students can become quite insular in pursuing their specialism and this lack of breadth and balance is not addressed within those programmes. The CP, however, makes a particular commitment to providing a broad and balanced education, making sure students communicate effectively and appreciate how to work with others while understanding the cultural differences they may experience. This is done in a way that provides the necessary skills for students to communicate their ideas in social contexts. Two Renaissance College students in the first CP cohort were shy individuals who found talking to others difficult; they have now become more eloquent and confident speakers who can talk passionately about their art. The CP provides a broad education within an IB framework and philosophy and, within it, the career-related study provides the students with an appropriate level of challenge to meet their career-related interests and talents.

Collaboration for sustainable Career-related Programmes

The case for the CP to produce educational change will rely on the commitment that all authorised IB World Schools make as they subscribe and adhere to the IB's standards and practices within a community of schools that shares and works together. If learning in the CP is to be personalised in an effective manner a wide range of options will be required to meet the needs of the students. The approach to implementing the CP that I am suggesting will go beyond the means and resources of a single school. However, through sharing career-related studies, together with the use of outsourced teaching (possibly including online courses), there is way for this to occur.

An important objective in achieving a wide variety of career-related studies for a student body is for schools to share the career-related studies they have established with external providers. This allows the schools to make available career-related studies which maybe only one or two students wish to pursue. Clearly, running a career-related offering in a school with one student is not sustainable, but pooling students would make far more options possible. It should be noted that this method is more suited to large cities with a sufficient number of IB schools and career-related providers. Nevertheless, online career-related courses could also provide schools in more remote locations with similar possibilities, and the sharing of information on these options could support a similar online CP community.

In a city which has several IB World Schools the key question will be: how can schools that compete for students share career-related studies? An answer is that the schools can still differentiate themselves by the career-related studies they offer, the quality of their CP core components and the approach and ethos of the school. The career-related study components that are outsourced are essentially educational programmes that a school can use in a similar way to the recently developed online DP courses (Pamoja Education) that allow schools that haven't got teachers, resources or the availability on the timetable to offer the course. In the case of the quality of these outsourced career-related studies, they should be consistent and of a high standard, regardless of which schools access them. It could also make sense for schools to share with other schools any in-house career-related offerings that they have developed as this could support low student numbers and help the school recoup costs. This could be beneficial to schools as it may prevent their students transferring to other schools to pursue the CP and their career-related study of choice.

This model for a group of CP schools in a city relies upon effective collaboration being established. Collaboration over scheduling is a very practical but important example. In Hong Kong, the majority of schools have completed most of their lessons before lunch and the optimum time for the career-related study options to be offered is in the afternoon. A typical school may have eight classes a day, and six of those classes usually occur before lunch. This makes it easier to schedule the DP courses that the CP students need, and the CP core components, in these six morning classes each day, allowing for the career-related study options to be scheduled in the afternoons. For schools to align their scheduling in this way can provide real sharing opportunities between schools, allowing students to travel to other schools for their career-related study. Collaboration between schools is also important with regard to external providers, as most will be reluctant to offer a course for one or two students. Schools sharing the provider can generate the number of students the provider needs to make the course viable. In some cases, providers are happy to offer their courses to one or two CP students who will join existing students from other programmes. That said, they would certainly be disposed to be even more flexible in terms of timetabling, and to open new classes, if they knew that their intake was to increase from a pool of CP schools.

Renaissance College has supported other schools in Hong Kong to become involved with SCAD, believing, as we do, in the potential of the CP to stimulate the creation of a community where schools can tap into a variety of providers. There are three schools in Hong Kong that are, at the time of writing, CP candidate schools and they are all going to offer SCAD as one of their CP career-related offerings. In turn the career-related options that they develop could then be shared, and we will have a connected and collaborative community that will be able to take full advantage of what the CP can offer.

The CP as a driver of change

At Renaissance College we have observed many valuable by-products of the CP. When a student completes a high school education before going on to further study or into a career, the change of learning environment can be dramatic. In a sense, an almost quantum leap takes place after school-based education has finished. The CP makes this transition less dramatic; the students know what to do and what to expect as their career-related study and skills development have prepared them well for this next stage in their lives. The development and experience that schools acquire from implementing the CP will help them support students to make this transition from traditional school settings to colleges and universities, where the learning experiences are more similar to those that students will experience professionally in their careers later in life.

The need for this change can also be seen in terms of gaining entry to universities in countries such as the US, where a shift away from admission based solely on academic performance has been seen for some time. The CP's structure provides more opportunities for internships, connections with industry, discussions with experts, and real-life experiences, and it is this involvement that provides the students with more experience and focused knowledge within their fields of interest. Students are likely to be able to talk in more detail about their specialism and have a more detailed and deeper understanding of the associated concepts and theories.

The CP can also influence teaching and learning across the whole school. It can provide the school with stronger links to other educational programmes, businesses and universities. The links that CP students make with local businesses and colleges can provide valuable connections in terms work experience, field trips and visiting speakers for the whole school. For example, as part of the collaboration between Renaissance College and SCAD, we have visiting lectures from SCAD for students outside the CP. SCAD has also provided expertise for events such as our fashion shows and design days. A CP designed around the hospitality industry could be good for catering for events and visitors at the school. A business-related CP could provide great opportunities for the CP students to consult with and advise students running businesses within the school.

Conclusion

The CP offers a wealth of possibilities for students that can be customised to meet their needs. The most efficient learning takes place when individuals are sufficiently challenged: not bored, where they lose interest, or over-taxed where they become anxious (Csikszentmihalyi, 1990). The area of sufficient challenge differs for individuals and this is where the personalised approach of the CP, from the variety of career-related studies to the number of DP courses that can be taken, allows for a customised programme, leading to meaningful career pathways for students that can give them an appreciable head start in their careers.

The CP is a promising educational model for the IB to offer to students in the last two years of high school, providing flexibility in the type and number of courses that a student can take. A caveat, as always, is that any educational programme has to be recognised by employers or colleges and universities to be of any use. Currently, the IB provides three choices for students in post-16 education: the CP, the DP and individual DP courses. The CP could be the first IB programme at post-16 level to offer flexibility at the level of the individual learner, with the IB's ethos and philosophy running throughout it.

Education will continue to change. The important question is will it just become a more refined model of the education developed during the industrial revolution or will it undergo a radical change in order to meet the needs of students, economies and societies in the 21st century? I hope it is the latter, and that the CP will provide the catalyst for the necessary paradigm shift.

References

Csikszentmihalyi, M. (1990): *Flow: the psychology of optimal experience.* New York City, NY: HarperCollins.

Kahneman, D. (2011): *Thinking, fast and slow.* London, UK: Allen Lane.

Nisbett, R. (2015): *Mindware: Tools for Smart Thinking.* London, UK; Allen Lane.

Pamoja Education: www.pamojaeducation.com

Robinson, K. (2015): *Creative Schools Revolutionizing from the Ground Up.* London, UK: Allen Lane.

Seligman, M. E. (2011): *Flourish: A New Understanding of Happiness and Well being and How to Achieve Them.* London, UK: Nicholas Brealey.

Chapter 16

From pilot to programme: the journey of the Career-related Programme

John Bastable

Introduction

The IB Career-related Programme (CP) was a vision founded on the ambitious hope of creating something that was felt to be missing for post-16 students: a career-related qualification. Now, a decade later and from the vantage point of the closing chapter of this book, the vision has become reality and a new realm of possibilities lies ahead. Writing this closing chapter to a book on the CP often felt more like opening the first chapter of a new story.

The stories in this book illustrate the remarkable distance the new programme has travelled in just a few years and I believe, along with the other writers in this book, that the CP will go a great deal further yet. There are several reasons for this belief, not least the recognition that the CP is a uniquely flexible programme, driven by the enthusiasm of creative practitioners, deeply concerned for the career needs of students and enhanced by a deep respect for the philosophy of the IB. Additionally, the world of education seems to be much more interested in career-related learning now than it was ten years ago. Changes in education and employment policies are leading towards a broader social acceptance of vocational learning which, coupled with student expectations of study programmes leading to gainful careers, places the CP in an advantageous position. I have enjoyed a long association with the IB. As the founding director of two IB World Schools, I was involved in the implementation of all four IB programmes. I was also privileged to contribute to the pilot group of schools which helped to develop the early model of the CP – known then as the IB Career-related Certificate, the IBCC. This final chapter combines some personal recollections of the development of the CP with reflections on the qualities of the programme recorded in this book which have brought the CP to its present exciting position on the cusp of educational change.

Serving students post-16

Many years ago in a conversation with George Walker, the inspirational educationalist and then Director General of the IB, I discovered that we both held concerns for those students who were unable to continue successfully to the IB Diploma Programme (DP). In this instance the concern was not due to the recurring accusation of the DP being elitist and beyond the means of poor students, but due to the observation that some students enrolling in the IB Primary Years Programme (PYP) and IB Middle Years Programme (MYP) were not all suited to the stringent academic requirements of the DP and would require something more vocational. Surely there had to be a way of opening a pathway for more students to enter the post-16 stage of IB education? The IB wanted to see many more students gaining access to an IB education but where were these students to come from and what could they study successfully? I mentioned to George that I had overheard a conversation between two young employees in a supermarket, which as I recalled went like this:

"My girlfriend's doing the IB."

"What's that?"

"It's like A Levels on steroids."

"No way we could do that then."

We wondered how we could enable young people entering the work force to be open-minded, lifelong learners and graduates from an IB programme. Instead, like these young adults stacking shelves, many students were denied access to the philosophy of the IB, embedded in the core of the DP: Creativity, Activity and Service (CAS), Theory of Knowledge (TOK) and the Extended Essay, the life-changing parts of the DP that provided students with the skills, knowledge and international mindedness to succeed in the global marketplace.

Much later, in a chance meeting at an IB conference, the above conversation was recounted to Monique Conn, the then Head of MYP, to which she replied, "Ah yes, Chris Mannix has been tasked to do something about that; he is here at the conference, you should talk to him." At the first opportunity I did just that and Chris outlined the work that had been initiated with some schools in Finland and Canada. These schools, as you will have read in Patrick Daneau's chapter, had been specifically chosen from national education systems with a proven commitment to vocational education. Chris also outlined the procedure for joining a pilot venture which was about to be launched. We went back to our school and with some enterprising teaching staff and supportive business associates we put together a programme in a very short time. The outcome was that we put Deira International School (DIS) in Dubai forward as a pilot school, and thankfully Chris accepted us. Chris Mannix sadly passed away in 2014 but he had been the undoubted champion of the CP, working tirelessly for its implementation and recognition. I suspect that many who knew him cannot imagine that the programme would have achieved its present shape and subsequent success without his enthusiasm, dedication and persistence.

For two years we worked with Chris and seven other pilot schools around the world to create a working CP curriculum. We met several times at the

IB's office in Cardiff to thrash out ideas, dispute content and shape policies. It seemed a constant struggle in those early days to unite all stakeholders in the project. The CP had to be defended from staunch supporters of the DP who, at that time, wanted it to be more academic, concerned that it might be perceived as lowering the standards and reputation of the DP. This conflicted with the view of CP practitioners who wanted something more practical. In his calm but determined manner, steering carefully between the many hazards that arose along the way, Chris succeeded in weaving together a CP curriculum that worked.

In the introduction to this book, Dominic Robeau has provided an excellent brief history of the CP and the early days of the steering group, the first cohorts of students, the many challenges they faced and the emergence of the IBCC in 2006 which, eight years later in 2014, became the CP. The pilot schools were all strikingly different. Coming from divergent educational backgrounds with disparate cultural and political obstacles to negotiate, both within the discussions and back in their host countries, theory and practice would often go in unexpected directions. What the participants had in common was a desire to offer a more meaningful high quality course of education to young people post-16 and beyond. We learnt a lot from each other and came to appreciate how many different ways there are to approach the same challenge, something which over time has made the CP such a flexible instrument. The delegates from those first pilot schools certainly had one common denominator: they were all dedicated educators and they felt they were on a mission. We shared a commitment to the philosophy of the IB, but recognised that although the academic rigour of the DP was not suited to all our students, its core, in essence, was.

Travelling from around the world we gathered in Cardiff on several occasions and the final meeting was hosted by Deira International School, in Dubai. David Barrs describes in his chapter how "Three colleagues were duly dispatched to the conference of pilot schools in Dubai (March 2010), itself a cause of some excitement for a state school whose professional development budget was, and still is, inadequate." The involvement of state-funded schools on the back of their own DP, or that of a sister DP school, would prove to be very important in the development of the CP and its subsequent growth. An IB education, originally developed for international schools and international students, could now be opened up to a much wider group of state-supported students.

During the pilot we wrote, "Deira International School was itself only two years old when the pilot began but was in the unique position of being owned by the Al Futtaim Group, a major Middle Eastern Company, which offered its considerable training and business services to help deliver and develop the vocational experience and training programmes" (Bastable and Bastable, 2009). For DIS it was the powerful linkage with the automotive and retail businesses which secured placements for our students and supported and validated the training programmes. Other institutions in the pilot were finding their own unique links between their communities and career-related pathways while engaging in such diverse programmes as police training and outdoor sports. Each one provided essential experience and evidence for the development of the programme, as well as finding the funding for it.

Challenges

A number of challenges quickly began to surface in the pilot schools. The career-related pathway of the CP sometimes conflicted with the perception of vocational courses held by parents, teachers and students. In an earlier chapter, Mike Worth writes that in one of the first parent information sessions he was asked: 'How does this get my son into university?' and further questions such as 'Is it accepted in other countries?' and 'Does it have equivalency?' These were the same questions all the pilot schools faced.

Initially, recruiting students to the new programme was almost as problematic as finding the funds to run it. Some affluent international parents felt their children were entitled to the best of higher education and saw the DP as the pathway to prestigious universities. In their eyes success was becoming a doctor or an engineer. To some we seemed to be peddling an easier vocational programme rather than pushing their students and ourselves a bit harder; they could tolerate work experience for perhaps a week, but not a full-time vocational programme. The same attitudes were to be found in state-funded schools in the UK at the time, although the government was once again beginning to encourage vocational education. In the US, the educational climate was somewhat warmer. Paul Campbell and Natasha Deflorian mention in their chapter that there was a growing concern and realisation that a four-year college path was not the best or only route for all students, and that vocational courses might offer something better. These slow changes in awareness would eventually lead to many schools taking up the CP in the US and the marvellous outcome of children from disadvantaged backgrounds gaining entrance to an IB education, as well as the financially privileged.

In those early days, however, it was a leap of faith to introduce the CP not knowing whether higher education institutions would accept the qualification, nor what sort of accreditation the IB could achieve for the CP. There were questions in each school concerning the level at which to pitch the entry requirements for the CP. It also appeared from the pilot schools' perspective that there was some reticence from within the IB itself about how many DP courses a student should study, and at which levels (Higher or Standard) in order to gain the CP award. The pilot schools held on to their High School Diplomas; it was too soon to throw them out! Then, as always, the CP coordinators really had their work cut out. Now, fortunately, the CP has answers to all these questions.

Successes

As the CP at DIS developed, I wrote to colleagues in the pilot group presenting them with the following observations and questions:

"Some anecdotal evidence is emerging that in schools running the pilot CP, the inclusion of CP students in DP CAS activities is having a positive effect on all the students. Would you agree?"

"The practical nature and enthusiasm of many CP students when given access to the IB core values for the first time, particularly through CAS and the CP Reflective Project, provides these pragmatic students with an opportunity to excel which they seem to accept with open arms. Is this true at your school?"

"We have found that DP students benefit immensely from the influx of enthusiasm and willingness of CP students to participate in this area. The CAS programme at DIS, for example is so vibrant, that some students from other non-IB schools in the area have asked to be allowed to volunteer for the activities. Have you any similar anecdotes to share concerning the impact of CP students on your school? If so, please let me know."

Following several replies I sent out a more formal Likert questionnaire to all the CP pilot schools. The results were subsequently published in the IS (International School) magazine (Bastable, 2011).

The survey revealed that the CP

- re-engages students who had thought their education had come to an end.
- exposes students to the IB philosophy, which would otherwise be denied them.
- leads to choices of more meaningful positions in the workforce and an alternative pathway to higher education.
- keeps open the inclusive education of the PYP and MYP
- enriches the school environment for those students in the DP

These positive, and sometimes unexpected, initial outcomes of the CP pilot project gave us great encouragement. Looking back at these early observations I am surprised and delighted to discover that they continue to ring true with the experiences of new schools offering the CP, as illustrated in this book. One important aspect of the CP which was not picked up in the survey, but quickly became apparent, was the importance of the the Reflective Project. Patrick Daneau remarks on the magic of this in his chapter when he writes, 'There is something fascinating and unique about the CP: it asks young students who are focused on and motivated by a career-related approach to education to reflect on an ethical issue.' This mandatory feature of the CP had been critical to the original vision for the programme, and the pilot schools spent many hours on it. Focusing on an ethical dilemma emerging from an issue in their career-related studies, demanded that students conduct a personal inquiry which called upon the skills and values that lay at the very core of the IB philosophy.

The first cohort of CP students from DIS received their awards in 2009 and Chris Mannix came to their graduation in Dubai as the guest speaker and representative of the IB. It was a very proud occasion for all present to see these first ever CP students graduate. They had done themselves, their school, their teachers and the IB proud. At the ceremony the CEO, Mr Al Futtaim, publicly announced that each of them was now eligible for a position in the Al Futtaim Group: there was a job for each of them if they wanted it. The career-related pathway was wide open.

How pleasing to read the reflections of Conan de Wilde, at one time the curriculum coordinator at the International School of Geneva, that some years later the effect continues: "The real success story lies in the transformation of CP students from passive, largely apathetic students with weak academic profiles, to learners who became deeply and actively involved in at least one facet of the school community".

The surprise was that these students, as if waking up from a long sleep, were now energised and committed; rather than being the reluctant learners they had been, they were all fired up to go into further education. Other contributors to this book have also recognised the phenomenon of the majority of CP students opting to continue into higher education before taking up their careers. The immediate challenge then appeared to be finding colleges and universities that recognised the new qualification and would offer appropriate courses. However, we all found that these students were snapped up! There were colleges and universities looking for students like these.

The CP had yet another unexpected effect. Some students at DIS declined a place on the DP to take the CP, not because of any perception of it being easier – some of the most academically able students opted for it – but because it was more suited to their future employment plans and academic pathways. They did not see the CP as easier or less academic, but rather as a course better designed for their needs than the traditional DP which had previously been their only option. Importantly, they now had a choice. Other writers, including Peter Kotrc and Julia Peters at Brandenburg International School in an earlier chapter, also record this phenomenon. This appeal to students who know what they want out of their education is one of the CP's abiding strengths.

There were rewards for teachers too. Many not only found writing units of work for the new programme stimulating, but more importantly they were now able to assist certain students to move forward in their education. Some educators, like certain writers in this book, had felt that their schools' inclusive mission statements fell short at the post-16 offerings in their schools, and indeed the mission of the IB itself. As a significant percentage of students in some schools either failed to obtain their DP award or were only allowed to take some DP subjects but not the full diploma, some of them left to attend other schools at the post-16 stage. With the CP there was a post-16 programme which offered to include many more of these students. As a direct consequence, the international schools which took up the CP found that they could now retain more of their students post-16. They also gained some additional students from groups of parents unhappy about sending their post-16 sons or daughters overseas; in the Middle East, sending teenage girls abroad for education is challenging for many families, thus the CP provided some gender equity as the girls could now continue in education in their home country.

Thankfully the IB found that the DP did not suffer from an undercutting of its academic rigour or reputation and, rather than lose by association with the CP, it has gained support. Schools without a DP programme are now allowed to become authorised to provide the CP. At the time of writing figures show the CP is going from strength to strength; there are 140 authorised CP schools, and a further 100 school are candidates to offer the CP.

At the close of this book it can be said that from small and tentative beginnings the CP has moved to being in the vanguard of career-related education globally. Able to change and adapt to local conditions and needs, it offers a plethora of post-16 pathways accessible to diverse groups of students hitherto denied an IB education. Its success is a great tribute to the visionaries who conceived it and the many teachers and school leaders who have contributed, and continue to contribute, to making it work. Personally, I believe it must be acknowledged that without Chris Mannix as one of the 'founding fathers' it would not be what it is. I think he would be absolutely thrilled with the way things are turning out, and delighted to read this book.

References

Bastable, J. and Bastable, J. (2009): 'A vocational course for the IB'. IS Magazine, ECIS, 12 (1).

Bastable, J. (2011): 'Expanding the vocational option'. IS Magazine, ECIS, 13 (3).

Glossary

A Levels – taken in England, Wales and Northern Ireland, and also worldwide, the **Advanced Level** is a qualification in a specific subject, typically taken by school students aged 16–18, at a level above GCSE. A Levels can lead to university, further study, training, or work.

BTEC – The **Business and Technology Education Council** in the UK ran the original BTEC award, introduced in 1984. A range of professional qualifications for students entering the workplace, progressing through their careers, or planning to enter university. Now awarded by the EdExcel examinations board, they are taken in more than 100 countries.

CP core components – Personal and Professional Skills, Service Learning, Language Development and the Reflective Project. The components are designed by the IB to support integration of the three parts of the CP.

EdExcel – an awarding body offering academic and vocational qualifications in schools in England, Wales and Northern Ireland and other countries. Now known as Pearson – London Examinations, it is a multinational education and examination body owned by Pearson.

EPQ – the Extended Project Qualification, is a stand-alone qualification taken by some students in the England, Wales and Northern Ireland, designed to be taken alongside A-levels. Typically, 5,000 words long it may also take the form of a film or performance.

GCSE – **General Certificate of Secondary Education**, a standard qualification in England, Wales and Northern Ireland, in a specific subject, typically taken by school students aged 14–16, at a level below A Level.

GPA – the **Grade Point Average** is the average result of all the grades achieved throughout a period of schooling or a degree. All grades from all classes are averaged to create a grade point average for the marking period.

Higher Level and Standard Level DP courses – two different levels of courses taken in the IB's Diploma Programme. To achieve a diploma, students must take typically three subjects at Higher Level, and three subjects at Standard Level. The levels are differentiated by the level of content in the courses.

IB Learner Profile – a list of ten attributes of lifelong learners: inquiring, knowledgeable, thinkers, communicators, principled, open-minded, caring, risk-takers, balanced and reflective. It embodies the IB's mission statement and is at the heart of all IB programmes.

IB World School – the title given to a school that is officially authorised by the IB to offer at least one IB programme

IGCSE – international version of GCSE (see above)

NUFFIC – the Netherlands organisation for international cooperation in higher education, it is an independent, non-profit organisation based in The Hague, Netherlands.

Project Lead The Way (PLTW) – a non-profit organisation that develops STEM (Science, Technology, Engineering and Mathematics) curricula for use by US elementary, middle, and high schools, and professional development training for instructors.

QCA – the **Qualifications and Curriculum Authority** is a London-based, non-departmental, public body which maintains and develops the national curriculum and associated assessments, tests and examinations, and accredits and monitors qualifications in colleges and at work.

Sixth Form – (also known as years 12 and 13) represents the final 1-3 years of secondary or high school in the England, Wales and Northern Ireland, where students, between 16 and 18 years of age prepare for their A Levels, or equivalent examinations.

TAFE – **Technical and Further Education**, a vocational education and training provider in Australia